Cucina Italiana
Comes to Brooklyn

Cucina Italiana
Comes to Brooklyn

John Agresto

An Italian-American Cookbook and Memoir

Cucina Italiana Comes to Brooklyn:
An Italian-American Cookbook and Memoir

Copyright © 2025 John Agresto

All rights reserved. No part of this book may be reproduced, stored in a retrieval system, or transmitted in any form or by any means— electronic, mechanical, photocopying, recording, or otherwise— without prior written permission from the publisher, except in the case of brief quotations used in reviews or critical articles.

Published by Casertavecchia Press
Santa Fe, NM 87505

ISBN: 978-1-945028-76-2 (paperback)
ISBN 978-1-945028-77-9 (hardcover)

Printed in the United States of America

Contents

Acknowledgments	xi
Preface	xv
Introduction	xix

Antipasti — 1

Italian Antipasto 1	3
Italian Antipasto 2	5
Bruschetta	7
Tomato Salad	7
Mozzarella and Tomatoes	8
Mozzarella and Oil	9
Melon and Prosciutto	10

Soup — 11

Chicken Stock	13
Beef Stock	16
Chicken Soup	17
Escarole Soup	19
Stracciatella, or Italian Egg Drop Soup	20
Stracciatella with Chicken	21
Escarole Soup with Beans and Tomatoes	21
Lentil Soup	22
Pasta Fazool	23
A Note on Writing in Books	24
Minestrone	25
Italian Clam Soup	26
Mussel Soup	27

Pasta 29

Pasta Fresca – Fresh Egg Pasta 32
Using the Pasta Machine 33
Pasta Fresca without Eggs 34
Cooking Pasta Fresca 35
Pasta Names 36
Caution 36
Sauces 37
Tomato Sauce 37
Tomato Sauce with Meat 39
Tomato Sauce with Meatballs 41
Tomato Sauce with Braciole 44
Tomato Sauce with Ground Beef 46
Tomato Sauce with Fresh Tomatoes 47
Red Clam Sauce 48
Tomato Sauce with Mussels 50
Tomato Sauce with Crabs 52
Tripe and Sauce 53
Tripe in Tomato Sauce 56
Baked Pasta with Tomato Sauces 57
Lasagna 57
Baked Ziti 60
Manicotti 61
Cannelloni 62
Other Pastas 65
Ravioli 65
Spinach and Cheese Filling for Ravioli 67
Gnocchi 67
Potato Gnocchi 68
Spinach Gnocchi 70
Pastina 70
A Note on Cheeses 71
A Note on Olive Oils 72
Pasta Sauces with Olive Oil 74
Aglio e Olio 74

A Note on Simplicity of Taste	75
Pasta with Broccoli Rabe	76
White Clam Sauce	77
Pasta and Squid	79
Linguini Tutto Mare	80
Pesto	82
Polenta	84
Cooking Polenta	84
Polenta with Gorgonzola	85
Polenta and Tomato Sauce	86
Polenta with Sausages 1	87
Polenta with Sausages 2	87
Fried Polenta	87
Risotto	88
More on Risotto: Peas, Asparagus, Porcini, Mushrooms, Shrimp ...	89
A Note on "White Foods"	92
Fish and Shellfish	95
Fish	97
Fried Fish Filets	97
Whole Baked Fish	99
Grilled Fish	100
Pan-Fried Whole Fish	101
Shrimp	101
Boiled Shrimp	103
Shrimp with Oil and Lemon	103
Fried Shrimp	104
Grilled Shrimp	105
Shrimp Scampi	106
Baked Stuffed Shrimp	107
Squid	110
Fried Squid or Calamari Fritti	112
Squid Salad	113
Baked Stuffed Squid	114

Baccala	116
Baccala Mantecato	117
Stockfish Salad	119
Baccala Fish Stew	119
Clams	120
Baked Stuffed Clams	120
Clam Broth	122
Meat, Chicken, and Eggs	123
Beef	125
Meatballs	126
Steak Pizzaiola	126
Steak with Olive Oil and Lemon	127
Chicken	128
Baked Chicken with Lemon	130
Chicken Cacciatore	131
Pork	132
Roast Pork	132
Sausage	135
Fried Sausages	140
Grilled Sausages	140
American Sausage	141
Veal	142
Veal Scaloppini (al Limone)	142
Veal Scaloppini Marsala 1	143
Veal Scaloppini Marsala 2	144
Veal Cutlets	145
Veal Ossobuco	146
Veal Parmesan	150
A Note on Wine	150
A Note on Salt	151
Eggs	152
Peppers and Eggs	153
Herbs and Eggs	154
Italian Sausage and Eggs	155

Vegetables	157
Artichokes	159
Asparagus	161
Fried Asparagus	161
Broiled Asparagus	163
Broccoli and Broccoli Rabe	164
Cold Broccoli with Lemon and Oil	165
Eggplant	165
Fried Eggplant 1	166
Fried Eggplant 2	167
Grilled Eggplant	167
Eggplant Parmesan	168
Fennel	170
Greens	171
Escarole, Endive, Dandelion, and Chicory	172
Greens, Garlic, and Oil	174
Greens and Beans	174
Ciccoria/Broccoli Rabe Water	176
Mushrooms	176
Fried Mushrooms	177
Baked Stuffed Mushrooms	178
Broiled Mushrooms	180
Peppers	181
Peppers and Onions	181
Roasted Red Peppers	183
Potatoes	184
Fried Potatoes	185
Boiled Potatoes with Olive Oil	185
Italian Potato Salad	186
Salads	187
Lettuce Salad	187
Mixed Green Salad	188
Tomato Salad	189
Salad with Gorgonzola	189
Pear and Gorgonzola	189

Spinach and Chard	190
Sautéed Spinach	191
Chard with Parmesan	192
Zucchini and Yellow Squash	192
Fried Zucchini	192
Zucchini Blossoms	193
Onion Tricks	195
Hints on Garlic	197
Growing Garlic	198
Pizzas and Calzone	201
Pizzas	203
Calzone	206
Easter Pie	207
Spinach Pie	210
"Italian Pancakes"	210
Desserts	213
Pastries	215
Cannoli	215
Cannoli Shells	216
Cannoli Filling	217
Zeppole	218
Fried Bows	219
Aunt Margaret's Ricotta Pie	220
Grain Pie	222
Chestnuts	224
Candied Orange Peel	226
Ice	227
Lemon Ice	227
Orange Ice	228
Conclusion	231
About the Author	233

Acknowledgments

The first person to suggest that I write a cookbook was the late Rainey Alford, a colleague of mine when I worked in D.C. He needed a recipe for tomato sauce, and from those two hand-written pages this book grew. It grew, to be honest, from memory and practice more than from any research. Which only means, as with all things Italian and male, the true beginnings of this book lie with my maternal grandmother, Maria DeBiagio. I probably spent as many hours with her, in her kitchen, watching her make sauce, or fry *zeppole*, or accidentally burn the garlic, as I did studying or playing.

Theresa Agresto, my late mother, took grandma's cooking, changed a few ingredients, standardized cooking times, and added that touch of '50's American simplification and technique to what was basically slow 1920's home cooking. If you look carefully, you'll see them both hovering over every page.

Then there were all the women in the neighborhood there in Red Hook, in Brooklyn, who never seemed unhappy to have me stand with them as they cooked, answering question after question: Comara Tessie, Aunt Margaret, Alice, Lucy, and Rae. I ate everything they put before me, even Alice's tripe.

My late wife, Cathy, always encouraged my cooking and seemed to enjoy every meal I made for her. Our daughters, Molly and Meghan, also liked everything I would make, except for anything containing eggplant.

I cannot begin to thank all the many friends who have eaten at my table, said good things about my cooking, and encouraged me to publish a book like this. Still, there is one person I want to acknowledge by name – John Shelton Reed. A scholar, a gentleman, a fine cook, and important cookbook author himself. He believed in this book even when I wasn't so sure. As to the rest of my friends, please know that I know who you are, that I have great affection for you, and I give you all my quiet thanks.

Adam Robinson, of Good Book Developers, shepherded this book through all the ins and outs of publishing with patience and professionalism. Thank you.

Thanks also go to my cousin, Judy Sabatino, who did the handwriting that begins each of the chapters.

A few years before my mother died, I collected every recipe I had written down on random scraps of paper and put together a book for her and for all her friends called *Tomatoes, Basil, and Olive Oil: An Italian-American Cookbook*. It was published by Wolfsbrunnen-Verlag, in Heidelberg, Germany, and I remain deeply thankful for their faith in the project. They not only said they would publish the book when no one else would, but they made that volume of recipes as appealing as any cookbook I have ever held. The book before you now is largely based on that original version and in it I have tried to preserve the character, the essence, of what made that book so special.

John Agresto
Santa Fe, New Mexico

Preface

"What kind of food do you usually eat?" my Italian-American doctor asked me years ago.

"Hot dogs, fries, hamburgers, steak, pork chops, cake ... You know, regular food."

"Now your grandparents, how long did they live?"

"Well, one was 96, another 93 ..."

"Did they eat butter?"

"No. I don't think it was even in the house."

"Good. Try to stay away from it, too."

"They drink much milk?"

"They never touched the stuff."

"Good. Leave it alone yourself. Did they eat much fish?"

"Sure, they ate a good bit of fish. Generally, cheap stuff — mussels, bluefish, mackerel, squid ..."

"Good, you do the same. Did they eat spaghetti?"

"Of course."

"Good. Then you can eat it too. Did they eat much meat?"

"Not much. They were poor. Sure, meat on Sunday, and maybe some chicken, or a few meatballs here and there."

"Good. On Sunday, eat some chicken. And, during the week, a few meatballs with the spaghetti won't hurt. How about beans, and lentils, and vegetables?"

"Sure, they ate them all the time."

"Good, you eat them all the time too."

"So, what's this? The new Remember Ellis Island Diet?"

"Look, you're 30 pounds overweight with a cholesterol level somewhere off the chart. You can eat like a poor Italian and maybe live to be 90, or you can eat like an American and say goodbye at 50. Vegetables, spaghetti, olive oil, fish ... there's no food that's better. Besides, everybody thinks we Italians are fat. We're really not fat, we're just short."

My doctor told me this about 45 years ago, and since then it seems that every week there's another news story about the beneficial effects of garlic, or the cancer-preventing qualities of tomato sauce, or even how olive oil might help prevent Alzheimer's. I half expect to read some day that broccoli rabe purifies the blood and dandelion greens ward off evil spirits. Then again, I have made it past 50.

While the book before you is, first and foremost, a cookbook, it is also a memoir of sorts, something of an amateur sociology text, and definitely an exploration of the centrality of kitchen and table to the Italian immigrant experience. I hope it gives readers a small insight into what it meant to grow up in an Italian-American family in New York — with, on every page, a steady emphasis on good food and cooking.

With that said, this isn't an encyclopedia of all the things Italians in urban America might have eaten over the years. Some of it no one will miss. I'm very fond of a maxim that I once read in an American cookbook, "If it can be poached, it can be fried." Well, the maxim in my neighborhood seemed invariably to be "If it can be cooked, it can be cooked in tomato sauce." As you might imagine, this brings about some very odd and forgettable recipes. For example, I simply refuse to give a recipe for hot dogs in tomato sauce. Or canned peas in tomato sauce. Or snails in tomato sauce.*

*Not only is eating snails boiled in tomato sauce gross, what we would do in preparation was even worse. You see, snails must be "purged" before you eat them. In grandma's house this involved washing the snails then putting the creatures in the bathtub, into which a little water and some shredded lettuce and perhaps some cornmeal was added. Of course, nothing prevented the little buggers from creeping out of the tub and all over the bathroom — floor, sink, you name it. So, each day, or twice and three times a day, you'd have to put them back in the tub and coax them to eat up the good stuff and get rid of the bad. This went on for three days or so. In the end, since they tied up the tub, the snails were no doubt cleaner than the rest of us. Sadly, the most appropriate day for Italians to eat snails is my feast day, June 24, the feast of John the Baptist. Still, someone would always buy me a Manhattan Special on my feast day, which helped a bit in counteracting the horror of *escargot a la tomato sauce.*

Introduction

Despite the fact that Italian cooking today is all the rage, there are virtually no books like this. All the truly fine Italian cookbooks available today approach Italian food from a point exactly opposite from this book. They have raised Italian cooking to the peaks of fine artistry. They have made it elegant, fancy, even delicate and subtle. Most have taken the cooking of northern and central Italy — Bologna, Florence, Rome — and used it as the highest example of great Italian cooking. And great it is. But it's not the cooking of the Italian-American experience in the New World.

This is a book that sets out the food we Italian-Americans ate growing up in the urban areas of America. It was, by and large, poverty food. At the time, of course, we didn't know it was poverty food. We thought kings ate stuffed pasta shells, and we ate like kings. We had spaghetti on Wednesday not because we were poor but because it was Wednesday.

Still, let me turn that statement around a bit: What we ate was surely the food of the poor; but to call it "poverty food" is to dishonor it and understate it. We took cornmeal and pork scraps and made polenta with sausages. We took boiled potatoes and made gnocchi. We took flour and water and made spaghetti and macaroni, manicotti and ravioli. We took the simplest and least expensive materials available to immigrants and transformed those ingredients into marvelous foods that were the center of Italian life. The food in this book is what made the kitchen and the table the center of Italian-American life for four and five stupendous generations. (I don't wish to overstate the matter, but this is the food Joe DiMaggio and Martin Scorsese ate.)

So, what I hope to accomplish in this book is to take the cooking that millions of Italian-Americans grew up with and reproduce it for the contemporary American kitchen. There are many true Italian dishes — everything from potatoes in cream sauce to baked larks and thrushes — that never made it to this country or into this book. This is, rather, a cookbook for those of us who grew up in Italian-American city neighborhoods, eating what was basically southern Italian cooking modified by the American marketplace. It is not a book to teach Americans how to prepare poached pears with zabaglione sauce. It shows you how to make a bowl of ziti like we had when we were young.

This means that the first people for whom this book is written are not serious chefs looking to expand their repertoire of exotic dishes. This book is for the millions of Italian-Americans who have left the Little Italys of our cities and fanned out over the country. It's an attempt not just to remind them of home, but also to help them recreate in the kitchen much of what they left behind.

Second, since the food is so good and so basic (and, to be honest, often so easy), I trust that non-Italians will find this book a useful addition to their kitchen shelves. In particular, I want to touch all those who think they're "cooking Italian" when they reach for that jar of already-prepared tomato sauce they bought at the supermarket. I want to help them see how easy, and how infinitely more delicious, preparing something simple, like real tomato sauce, can be.

To do both these things — to reach the last generation or two of Italian-Americans and to introduce others to the simplicity and greatness of basic Italian-American cooking — this has to be a book that's easy to read, interesting to read, and helpful at every turn. This is not a book of recipe after recipe. It's a book, I hope, that explains what we're doing, the principles of what we are doing, on each page.

Because I dislike all cookbooks that are full of instructions and not explanations, I've tried to go slow, explain the why and not just the how of each food, and do it in a way that's engaging as well as informative. This is partly why each recipe is a narrative and not just a list of ingredients followed by directions. I have faith that anyone can read a few paragraphs, understand them, and then put a dish together without the kind of detail needed to build the next Mars probe. So, I hope I've written in a way that what is done is understood and not just followed. Besides, this food is pretty simple. As I've said, that's partly why it's so good.

Although I know that many Italian-American men think that cooking is best left either to restaurant chefs or to women, I can't let them get away with that. I've intentionally tried to make this a cookbook accessible to men, no matter how inept they think they are. Honestly, most Italian-American men are probably good enough at basic cooking. At least, if your growing up was anything like mine, there was usually someone around you cooking almost all the time.

So, guys, I've written this book to show you that if you can grill sausages then, dammit, you can make sausages. Moreover, by now most children and grandchildren of immigrant Italians have married non-Italians – people who think that gnocchi might be the abbreviation of the Albanian secret police. So, if you want a grain pie, or some homemade cannoli, you're going to have to read this book, put on an apron, and start cooking. If nothing else, it will make your mother happy.

Antipasti.

Antipasti

Large, festive meals would always begin with something to eat before the pasta was served — hence, antipasto. (No, it doesn't mean something contrary to pasta; it means something you eat before you tackle the rest of the meal: sort of like hors d'oeuvres, except everybody sits down to eat it instead of standing around, nibbling on small portions, and acting sophisticated.)

While there are many wonderful ways of beginning an Italian meal, in the old neighborhood only one or two dishes actually went by the name "Italian Antipasto." Let's begin there; then move on to other equally fine antipasti.

Italian Antipasto 1

Begin by making a dish of Tuna and Beans (Tonno con Fagioli) that will be the centerpiece of the antipasto platter:

Drain and rinse two small (15oz.) cans of cannellini beans (Italian white kidney beans). Set them aside. Next, prepare a modified Italian dressing: Into a bowl containing 1/2 cup fragrant olive oil, add 1/2 teaspoon of salt, a grinding of black pepper, and either two tablespoons fresh lemon juice or two tablespoons red wine vinegar: Whisk this all together.

Now add either four scallions (including part of their green tops) finely chopped, or one small onion, finely chopped. Whisk this together as well. Pour the dressing over the beans, mix it all lightly with a fork, and set the beans aside for at least an hour to let the flavors meld. If it seems dry, add more oil and lemon juice or vinegar. Then, gently, mix into the beans one or two well drained cans of tuna in oil.

Set this mix of tuna and beans in the center of a serving platter. Surround the tuna with bright, crisp leaves of lettuce.

Now, finely chop three stalks of celery and four or five roasted red peppers packed in oil. You can use store-bought peppers in oil if you must, but peppers roasted and prepared at home are better.

To this add a dozen or more chopped green olives and a dozen or more chopped black olives. If you have more scallions, finely chop three or four, including some of their green tops, and add them as well. If the mix seems dry, drizzle some olive oil over the top. You now have a delicious mix of celery, scallions, peppers, and olives.

Place this evenly around the tuna and beans, on the lettuce leaves. Garnish the platter with lemon wedges and sprinkle a small handful of chopped Italian parsley over it, or at least over the tuna. Serve at room temperature.

If you want to begin with dried beans rather than canned, start with about a cup and a half of white kidney, great northern, or navy beans. Put them in a pot with water to cover by about two inches and bring them slowly to a simmer. Simmer them for about five minutes; then set the pot aside for an hour, so the dry beans will begin to absorb the water. After an hour, put the beans back on the stove, add more water to be certain the beans remain covered while they simmer, and cook them gently for another hour and a half or two. When done, the beans should be soft, but their skins should still be intact.

Drain them thoroughly and, while still warm, mix them with the oil and lemon juice dressing. Proceed as above.

Tuna and beans, without the celery-olive-pepper mix, is wonderful in and of itself, either as a small antipasto or as a nice lunch. Eat it with crackers or crusty bread.

Italian Antipasto 2

This antipasto is like the first, but it builds on cold cuts rather than tuna and beans.

In the center of a large platter, slice a pound of fresh mozzarella cheese, salt it lightly, drizzle some olive oil and snip a few sprigs of fresh basil over the top. Around the mozzarella, decoratively place a half pound of thinly sliced prosciutto, a half-pound of sliced salami or capicola, and perhaps a half pound of mortadella. If you can, try rolling them, or folding them into triangles. If you have some perfectly ripe tomatoes, slice them into wedges, salt them slightly, coat them very lightly with olive oil, and snip some basil over them. Surround the cold cuts with the tomatoes then surround the tomatoes with wedges of hard-boiled eggs.

You can stop here or go on. For example, you could add the celery, olive, pepper, and scallion mix, or some variant of it, from the first recipe. Perhaps you might set these down on fresh lettuce leaves. You could add slices of roasted red peppers, or store-bought artichoke hearts that you've rinsed, drained, and set to marinate in oil with a squeeze of lemon. Some rinsed and dried anchovy filets could be added or, better yet, use those whole anchovies packed in oil. Use your imagination, stopping short of pineapple wedges.

How one mixes or keeps separate on the fork the various elements in an antipasto determines the taste of each bite. Italian antipasto: what a remarkable invention!

Bruschetta

A bruschetta is simply a thick piece of Italian bread, toasted or grilled, then topped with anything from garlic and olive oil to chopped tomatoes and basil to grilled red peppers.

Cut slices of fresh Italian bread at least one-half inch thick and toast them lightly under the broiler or, better yet, brush them with olive oil and grill over a charcoal fire. When done, they should be more golden than brown.

This can now be topped with nothing more than a drizzle of olive oil, or with some minced garlic heated in oil. Or you can make a tomato salad (below), chopping the tomatoes finer than you usually would for a salad and covering the toast with that. You might want to spice up the tomatoes by adding a few capers or chopped green and black olives. Or you can cover each slice liberally with roasted red peppers that you've put aside in oil, with some coarse salt over the top.

Tomato Salad

This could serve as either an antipasto before the meal or as a simple salad after. It also exemplifies a few interesting things about food — first, nothing's better than simple; second, since tomatoes and basil necessarily go together, why God first planted basil in the East but grew tomatoes in the Americas is a great mystery.

Wash one just-ripe tomato per person and cut each into wedges, slices, or pieces. Salt and pepper the tomato and add about a quarter cup of fragrant olive oil for every four tomatoes. Snip or tear onto this five or six fresh basil leaves and toss. A little wine vinegar is sometimes added, but that just starts you down the road to complications.

Mozzarella and Tomatoes

In summer, one of the simplest of first courses, and one of the finest, is mozzarella and tomatoes. Its fineness depends, however, on the quality of both ingredients. Use only fresh mozzarella and the summer's best tomatoes. If you must use either commercial plastic-sealed cheese, or less-than-perfect tomatoes, make something else.

Preparing this dish is simplicity itself. Cut the ball of cheese into slices about a quarter-inch thick. Cut ripe yet firm tomatoes into an equal number of slices, also a quarter-inch thick. Plum tomatoes tend to be too dry for this dish; regular "beefsteak" tomatoes are better.

On a bed of washed and dried lettuce leaves, alternate the slices – one tomato, one mozzarella – around the edge of the dish, spiraling into the center. Or arrange parallel rows down a small oblong platter. Drizzle about two tablespoons of olive oil over the layers, scatter five or six shredded basil leaves over the top, add a few grindings of black pepper, a light sprinkle of salt, and it's done.

This can be served at the table as an antipasto, as an hors d'oeuvre with slices of French bread, or as a salad with or after the main meal.

Mozzarella and Oil

This makes for a great light lunch or antipasto. Again, use fresh (and only fresh) mozzarella cheese. Everyone knows that mozzarella slices easily. Some people also know that it grates passably well on the shredding holes of a cheese grater. What most people do not know is that it also "strings" very nicely. That is, it can be pulled apart into long, thread-like pieces. Each ball of fresh mozzarella has a "grain," so to speak, and you can "unravel" the cheese by pulling off strips along the grain. Start at the outside and pull quarter-inch wide strips off the outer edge. Each strip will be about an inch to two inches long. Continue until you've pulled off or "stringed" as much cheese as you need.

Place the stringed cheese in a bowl, drizzle a small amount of good olive oil (just enough to give it a taste; not enough to cover it or drown it), grind black pepper and sprinkle salt lightly over the top, garnish with parsley or snipped basil, mix and eat. To make this even more festive, surround the mozzarella with chopped, fresh tomatoes in summer, or roasted red peppers in the fall. Or, on a small platter, you could put roasted red peppers at one end, cooked green peppers at the other, mozzarella in the middle. Yes, it's corny, it looks like the Italian flag, but it sure tastes good.

Melon and Prosciutto

In summer, when melons are at their peak, serve this before dinner. The sweetness of a ripe melon and the saltiness of the prosciutto are wonderful together.

Buy a ripe, fragrant melon – cantaloupe, honeydew, or one of the many variations on them around these days. Cut into wedges and remove the skin. On individual plates place one wedge of melon covered with paper-thin slices of prosciutto. Garnish with slices of lime and eat with a knife and fork. Like virtually all Italian antipasti, this is served at room temperature, not cold.

If you can manage to get perfectly ripe figs they can substitute for the melon any day.

Soup

Before we tackle soups, let's begin with making stocks.

Chicken Stock

There seems to be hardly a cuisine on earth that doesn't use chicken stock. Actually, in thinking about the sauces of France or the soups of the Orient, the Greeks, or the Jews, it might be that Italians use chicken stock less than they should. Nonetheless, for escarole soup, for braising fennel, or for stewing up some bitter greens, nothing is finer. Here's how to make it:

The most economical way to make stock is to ask the butcher for a few pounds of chicken scraps — backs, necks, bones — in any combination. Buy, say, three to four pounds. Wash them all thoroughly in a basin of tepid water, discarding any large bits of stray fat. (If there's any off smell to the pieces, throw them all out and ask for your few dollars back.)

Put the pieces in a large pot with enough water to cover them completely by an inch or two and, over medium heat, bring the chicken to a simmer. A brown scum will slowly start to form over the top. Skim this off with a slotted spoon. Don't worry if you don't get every last bit; it's not harmful in the least, only ugly. Often, if the truth be known, I don't bother skimming at all — I just let these coagulated proteins stay behind, stuck to the chicken's skin when I strain the stock at the end.

Into this slowly simmering broth add a peeled and chopped onion, a peeled and chopped carrot or two, a few sprigs of Italian parsley, a tablespoon of coarse salt, half a dozen or more peppercorns, a bay leaf, perhaps some thyme, maybe a tablespoon of fennel or anise seed (or a few pieces of star anise, which is hardly authentic, but good). Leeks can be added or substituted for the onion; a few cloves of garlic can go in as well. In moderation, everything adds a flavor note to the broth. Just don't get too carried away and have it wind up tasting like spice-shelf soup.

Let this simmer for about three hours or a bit more. Taste it for salt as it cooks down, remembering that, while water evaporates, salt concentrates. You can always add more salt later.

After three hours, strain the broth into a bowl through a colander, pressing the vegetables lightly with the back of a spoon to get out a few last drops of taste. After simmering all these hours, the chicken parts are fairly well spent. You can dig out the few pieces of meat you can find and sprinkle them with salt and eat them over by the sink, but they won't have much flavor.

Skim as much fat as you can from the top of the bowl, taste for salt, and freeze in plastic containers whatever you won't use within a day or two. Chicken stock freezes beautifully, and virtually forever. How do you know when to make more? When you look in the deep freeze and see only one or two containers left.

If you don't use chicken parts and wish to cook a whole bird for stock, this is fine, too. Buy yourself a fairly hefty chicken, perhaps four to five pounds, wash it, cover it with water, bring it to a slow simmer, skim it, then add the herbs and salt and vegetables (as above). However, since if you cook the whole bird for the allotted three hours, all the best parts — the breast, the thigh meat — will dry out and turn the consistency of dime store halvah, I remove the chicken from the stock just as the breast and thigh are done (about 40 minutes), slice off the breast and thigh meat, set them aside, and return the sad-looking carcass to the pot for the remainder of its three long hour simmer. There's still plenty of meat on the chicken to give you a fine stock, and now you have some perfectly poached chicken to make a small chicken salad or to add to whatever soup or stew you might care to make.

Beef Stock

Although in my experience beef stock is used less than chicken stock, it, too, is a very handy base for some of the best Italian soups.

In my opinion, bones with some of meat attached make the very best stock. So, in an eight quart or larger pot, brown three or four pounds of beef shin bone, ribs, or whatever the butcher might have that's inexpensive. Though browning these bones in the pot you will cook them in is usually the most convenient, sometimes you might prefer to brown them in a hot (400°) oven instead. If so, just put them in the pot after they've browned up nicely.

To the meat and bones add two quarts of water and a small handful of salt. Bring the bones to a simmer and skim off any scum that rises to the surface. When the scum is mostly gone, add an onion, a few cloves of garlic, a stalk or two of celery if you have it, and a carrot — all roughly chopped. You might also add a bay leaf and a few sprigs of parsley. Often, I brown the vegetables first, since I think it gives the stock a better color and a richer flavor, but this really isn't necessary.

After about an hour, or when the meat seems cooked and tender, remove the bones, take the meat off them, set the meat aside, and put the bones back in the pot. Simmer the bones slowly for a minimum of three to four hours all totaled. Continue to add water if it seems to boil away, though the pot should be partially covered and the heat very low.

After three or four hours, strain the stock, skim off much of the grease and oil on top, and discard the spent vegetables. You now have some wonderful stock to use in soups such as minestrone, and even some meat to add as well.

This will keep in the refrigerator for a few days and freeze perfectly well indefinitely.

Chicken Soup

In some ways, soups are the hardest to write up as recipes since they are quintessentially inexact. Think of soups as snowflakes — try as you might, you will never make the same one twice. At best, soup recipes are just guidelines, or perhaps a written picture of what the result should look like. In this case, what you want are tender pieces of chicken and bright vegetables sitting in clear, steamy liquid with the aroma of just-grated Parmesan floating over the top.

Begin with a very rich, full-flavored chicken stock that you made yourself. Resist the temptation to recycle the chicken meat you used to make the stock. If the stock is well made, this chicken is spent. So, take your best stock, say a cup to two cups per person (depending on whether the soup will be the whole meal or not), and slowly simmer in it some new chicken — perhaps a breast or two.

After this has started to re-simmer, skim the top and add a few carrots, peeled and cut into rounds or half-inch chunks, a chopped onion, and a stalk or two of chopped celery. If you'd like some potato in the soup, or perhaps some pasta, cook these separately in boiling salted water and add them at the end. This is simply a matter of aesthetics, since cooking potatoes or pasta in the stock will cloud it up. (For pasta, if that's what you choose, pick something small, like orzo.)

What you now have is stock simmering with chicken and vegetables, with, perhaps, potatoes or pasta cooking on the side. (Drain the potatoes or pasta as soon as they're done and set aside.) When the chicken is just done, perhaps in 25 or 30 minutes, remove it from the stock, let it cool, discard the skin and bones and cut the meat into strips or small chunks. If it needs another minute or two of cooking, put it back in the pot; otherwise parcel the meat out to the various bowls.

Add to this the potatoes or pasta, if you made it, then ladle on the still simmering stock with its vegetables. Stir into each bowl a bit of chopped Italian parsley and grate a few tablespoons of Parmesan over it all. And it's done.

We added the parsley at the end not so much for taste as for color since, as you can see, there's very little color in this soup other than for the bright orange of the carrots. What I often do to remedy this is to cook up some well-washed spinach leaves (or, these days, some thawed frozen spinach) in simmering salted water, shock them under cold water, shred them, and add them to the bowl just before I ladle on the simmering stock. The whiteness of the meat and potatoes, the orange of the carrots, and the green of the spinach all make for a visual delight. Never overlook the aesthetic possibilities of food. It may just be chicken soup, but there's no reason for it not to be beautiful chicken soup.

Escarole Soup

This is simplicity itself, and the basis of a number of soups that follow.

First, wash one head of escarole, discarding any hard core. Simmer for 15 minutes in salted water. Drain, chop very coarsely, and rinse under cold, running water. (As I've noted elsewhere, running green vegetables under cold water after cooking them "sets" a bright green color. If you don't do this the greens will tend to turn a shade of olive gray. This doesn't affect the taste at all, it's just not as pretty.)

Bring a quart of good, homemade chicken stock to the simmer and cook the parboiled escarole in it for another 15 minutes, or until tender. Ladle into individual bowls and stir into each a handful of freshly grated Parmesan cheese. If you'd like, drizzle some olive oil over each soup. You should serve it with crusty French or Italian bread. In fact, if the bread is too stale to eat on the side, place a slice or two in the bowl and put the soup and cheese over it.

You might notice, when we get to dandelion greens later, that preparing those greens bears more than a passing resemblance to this soup. There are two reasons for this. First, the line between a bowl of soup and a plate of cooked greens is sometimes hazy — the more stock you add to a dish the more that same dish goes from merely cooked vegetables to soup. Second, escarole, dandelion, chicory greens, endive, Belgian endive, radicchio and, yes, lettuce, are all family related. Some grew up cultured, some grew up wild, and some (like lettuce) were cultivated to be so refined that much of the earthiness and bitterness has been bred out of them. But, in truth, all of them can be called "ciccoria" and cooked as escarole soup, though radicchio will always go from a pretty red to a pale gray-green no matter what you do to stop it.

Stracciatella, or Italian Egg Drop Soup

This is the same soup as above, with the addition of egg. Simply whip two or three eggs with a tablespoon or two of water. Just before you're ready to serve the soup, with the stock at a simmer, drizzle the eggs slowly over the top of the soup. The hot stock will cook the eggs virtually immediately. (Of course, you can salt and pepper the eggs before adding them to the soup but don't, as some cookbooks recommend, add the cheese to the eggs. It makes for a curdled, ugly mess. Put the cheese on top of each bowl of soup and stir in.)

Stracciatella with Chicken

Now we're going from a soup to a one-course meal. Before adding any greens to your stock, simmer one or two chicken breasts in the stock for about 30 minutes. Count on one side of a full breast to feed two people. When the meat is done, remove it from the stock and let it cool. You should now add the parboiled and chopped escarole to the still-simmering stock.

While the soup is bubbling away with its escarole, discard the skin and bones from the breasts, and either cut the meat into cubes or pull it into small strips. When the soup is just about done, return the meat to the pot to heat through. (If the meat wasn't perfectly done when you removed it from the stock, let it sit in the simmering soup for a minute or two to cook further.) Drizzle the beaten eggs into the soup just as in the previous recipe. Again, serve with grated Parmesan cheese and bread.

Escarole Soup with Beans and Tomatoes

This is, to put it plainly, a beautiful, delicious peasant soup. It is also simplicity itself.

Wash and core a large head of escarole, discarding any wilted or blemished leaves. Parboil the leaves in a large pot of boiling, salted water for about 15 minutes; then discard the water, run the leaves under cold water, drain them and chop.

While the escarole is simmering, drain and rinse one can of white cannellini beans (also called white kidney beans). Put the beans into a quart or more of slowly simmering homemade chicken stock. Peel, seed and chop roughly a few Italian plum tomatoes. (You can easily peel the tomatoes by dropping them into the water in which the escarole is parboiling.) If you need to, you can use canned, peeled tomatoes in place of fresh. Depending on personal taste, three or four tomatoes will do, but more rarely hurt anything. Add the chopped cooked greens and the chopped tomatoes to the soup and simmer for another 15 to 20 minutes.

Serve with grated Parmesan cheese, a drizzle of olive oil, and some solid, crusty bread.

Lentil Soup

There are as many variations on lentil soup as there are people – or perhaps even more, since I doubt anyone has ever made it the exact same way twice.

Pick over one pound (about two cups) of lentils, discarding any debris the lentil pickers might have picked. Wash the lentils in a sieve or colander until the water runs clear.

Chop two large onions, three carrots, two or three celery stalks, and three cloves of garlic. Put these in a large pot or saucepan and either add two quarts of homemade chicken stock or sauté all these chopped vegetables for a few minutes in olive oil and then add the two quarts of chicken stock. If you have a piece of pork rind, you can add that as well. Bring the stock and vegetables to a simmer and add the washed lentils. Cook gently for about a half hour, or until the lentils are tender but not disintegrated. With a few slices of Italian or French bread, this makes a good meal all by itself.

With ham: If you have some pieces of smoked ham or a small hambone, use that to flavor the lentil soup. Begin with two quarts or more of water and simmer the ham or bone until the water has picked up its flavor. Then shred the ham or discard the bone and proceed as above, eliminating the piece of pork rind.

Be careful salting this stock, since the ham may have salted the water enough.

Pasta Fazool

Everyone has heard of pasta e fagioli, but mostly they've heard of it as "pasta fazool." "Pasta e fagioli" simply means macaroni and beans, even if "pasta fazool" sounds like a rude comment involving personal body parts. In a large saucepan or stockpot, sauté two onions and three or four chopped cloves of garlic in a quarter cup of olive oil. As the onions start to become translucent, add one small can of tomato paste to the oil. Rinse out the can with a few tablespoons of water and add that to the pot. Stir this all together. After a minute or two add a generous eight cups of chicken stock to the pot – or, back in the day, water if it was Friday. As this begins to simmer add a tablespoon of dried oregano, a teaspoon of salt (more if you used water), some grindings of black pepper, and one can of white cannellini beans, rinsed and drained. Cover and let this simmer gently for half an hour.

Meanwhile, cook a quarter pound of small, tubular macaroni, perhaps tubetti or ditali or even elbow macaroni, in boiling salted water. When done, add this to the soup, cook everything together for a few minutes, and serve in warm bowls with a generous amount of grated Parmesan.

This is obviously a fairly basic way to cook this dish. Variations abound. If you want it heartier, make a note in the margin of this book to use two cans of cannellini beans instead of one. Or use more pasta. Some people thicken this by cooking the pasta right in the soup. And you could always give it more of a tomato flavor by also putting in half a can of crushed tomatoes, or even some already prepared tomato sauce.

A Note on Writing in Books

Who invented the notion that it's wrong to write in books? I even know people who cover their open cookbook with clear plastic so that not one drop of stray pizza sauce will ever disgrace the purity of their pages. I'm here to tell you this is wrong. If you love a book, you should write in it. If you use a book – which is why it was written in the first place – you will get things on it.

So, please, write away. If the recipe for pasta fazool is too thin for your taste, or needs more salt, or if you want to try using dried beans instead of canned, don't rely on your memory, write it down! Note it in the margin. Cross out the offending ingredient. Write "This is wonderful!" at the top of the page. It's the only way, really, to show the book you care.

Minestrone

Rather than "big soup," I always thought minestrone meant "soup made of things left over in the fridge." If you approach it with that attitude, it will keep you from fretting too much about exact ingredients.

At its heart, minestrone is a vegetable soup, usually in a beef broth, and usually including not only beans and tomatoes but also root vegetables, green vegetables, zucchini, and a bit of pasta as well. The exact ingredients and their exact proportions are left to your ingenuity and, as I say, the contents of the refrigerator.

Into two quarts of homemade beef stock add a small (15 oz.) can of drained and rinsed cannellini beans or a drained and rinsed can of red kidney beans, one or two potatoes cut into large dice, two zucchini cut into 1/2 inch dice, two stalks of roughly chopped celery, a few cloves of chopped garlic, two or three chopped carrots, one large chopped onion and either four or five peeled chopped fresh plum tomatoes or a small can of peeled Italian plum tomatoes, cored and chopped. Once the potatoes are on their way to being done, add either a bunch of washed and chopped spinach leaves or a small head of escarole, parboiled and chopped. Then add about a half-cup of small, tubular macaroni, like ditali or tubettini.

When the soup is nearly done (which means the beans are soft and the potatoes tender and the pasta al dente), add any scraps of cooked beef you have left over from making the beef stock. Serve in hot bowls covered with a good handful of freshly grated Parmesan cheese.

Any number of variations are possible. First, in place of beef stock feel free to use either chicken or vegetable stock. (Vegetable stock being nothing more than lightly salted water in which mild vegetables have been cooked until they've released their flavor.) Second, chick-peas (garbanzo beans) are as authentic in minestrone as cannellini or kidney beans. Third, green beans, peas, beet greens, cabbage, leeks, and Swiss chard can all appear in the soup, as can chopped basil instead of cheese as a garnish. You can even substitute a half cup of cooked rice for the pasta at the end. Perhaps the only guideline is that there should be a fairly even balance between beans, greens, vegetables, and the starches, whether the starches are potatoes, pasta, or rice.

Italian Clam Soup

With the addition of a few potatoes, this sometimes goes by the name of Manhattan clam chowder. Unlike New England clam chowder, which has a cream and butter or salt pork base, this soup (or chowder) relies on tomatoes and olive oil.

Drain, core, and chop enough canned plum tomatoes to make about two cups. In a half-cup of olive oil gently sauté three large cloves of garlic, mashed or chopped. When the garlic is ever so lightly colored, add the prepared tomato pulp. Cook this on the lowest flame for about 10 minutes, stirring often so that nothing scorches. After 10 minutes, add a generous two cups of water and let it all bubble gently while you prepare the clams.

In another pan with a tight-fitting lid put either a quarter-cup of olive oil or quarter-inch of water. Set the pan on medium heat and add two dozen small hardshell clams, thoroughly washed and scrubbed. Cover the pan and regularly shake it back and forth to encourage the clams to open. As the clams open, remove them with tongs or a slotted spoon and put them into four individual heated bowls. Discard any clams that refuse to open after five minutes or so.

Strain the clam broth into the bubbling tomato sauce, cook it for a second; then pour the broth over the clams in the bowls. Garnish with chopped parsley and eat it with crusty bread.

Mussel Soup

This is similar to the clam soup discussed above.

Drain, core, squeeze, and chop enough canned plum tomatoes to make about two cups. In a six-quart saucepan, heat a half-cup of olive oil. Gently sauté one small onion, finely chopped, a pinch or two of red pepper flakes, and two stalks of celery, also finely chopped. When the onion becomes translucent, add three or more cloves of garlic, mashed or chopped. As soon as the garlic begins to take on color, add the prepared tomato pulp. Cook this gently for about 10 minutes; then add two or more cups of water. Simmer this all together while you prepare the mussels.

Wash three or four dozen mussels under tepid water, nudging the shells of each one back and forth to be certain they're closed tight. Debeard each one and discard any that are open and will not shut when roughly handled. (Debearding is easy. Using your thumb and a small paring knife lift the beard up and away from the shell. Soon it should pop off the muscle of the mussel, so to speak. In any event, don't be concerned if some of the beard stays attached, it's merely a protein filament that the mussel uses to attach itself to a rock or piling; eating it is perfectly OK.)

Now, put the clean mussels into the tomato soup and cover the pan tightly. Every so often give the pan a shake to encourage the mussels to open. After four or five minutes, see if the mussels have all opened. If there are still a few recalcitrants left, cook the soup a while longer. After a few more minutes, remove and discard any mussels that have failed to open, divide the soup into four bowls, and garnish with chopped Italian parsley or perhaps a bit of chopped fresh basil. As always, have crusty bread with your soup.

Pasta

Pasta

Pasta virtually defines Italian cooking in the general American mind. And, until a few years ago, dried pasta from a box was pretty much the totality of what most Americans used. Then people began to discover "fresh" pasta, and a whole mythology grew up around it. It started to be believed that fresh pasta was better and more authentic than good ol' dried pasta.

Well, while I'd be the last to disparage the virtues of homemade fresh pasta, this is really the case where the two products are simply different, not better or worse. Indeed, when it comes to blending with sauces and holding sauces better, dried pasta, which can have a rougher texture when cooked than fresh pasta, often has a leg up.

Although we grew up primarily with dried pasta — pasta secca, or, more usually, past'ascuitta — occasionally we'd turn out some fresh pasta, pasta fresca. We didn't do this all that often, probably because the best place we had to let the fresh pasta set was on a sheet over my uncle's bed, which forced him to nap on the sofa, which I don't think he cared for all that much.

Nonetheless, let's begin this chapter with putting together our own homemade fresh pasta.

Pasta Fresca – Fresh Egg Pasta

Semolina flour, otherwise known as durum wheat flour, is made from hard wheat and has a higher gluten content than regular, "all-purpose" flour. Semolina makes a somewhat more elastic dough than regular flour and thus a finer final product, one that cooks up better, with a firmer, chewier texture when done. (At the opposite end from semolina is cake flour, which is made from very soft wheat. Great for cakes, lousy for pasta.) You can use "all-purpose" flour if you can't find semolina and you'll still be pleased with the results.

A pasta machine will make even, precise, perfectly cut fresh pasta, but it's not appreciably better or faster than making it by hand. Let's begin with handmade rather than machine-made pasta fresca, this one with eggs.

Mound four cups of semolina on a spotlessly clean table or countertop. Make a deep well in the center, like a miniature volcano, and add four beaten eggs, a half teaspoon of salt, a quarter-cup of warm water, and one tablespoon of olive oil. Mix this all together with your fingertips; then start to knead it with the palm and heel of your hands. Knead it together for about 10 minutes, adding slight amounts of semolina if either your hands or the countertop gets too sticky. Soon, the semolina will lose its grainy, sugary character and start to look and feel like regular dough. After 10 minutes of kneading, form the dough into a ball and let it rest for another 10 minutes.

After the dough has rested, divide it into four parts. Roll out each piece on the surface where you were just working. Roll them into sheets as thin as you can make them. Now, with a sharp knife, cut the flattened piece of dough into noodles anywhere from 1/4 to 1" wide. Set them aside on a clean cloth to dry for one hour. Four cups of flour will make a little over a pound and a half of fresh pasta.

Using the Pasta Machine

A pasta machine not only cuts the pasta into perfectly even widths, it also kneads the dough for you. Use the same recipe for egg pasta given above. After you've mixed all the ingredients and started kneading the dough with your hands, stop, and divide the dough into four or more pieces. Let them sit and rest for a few minutes. Then, with the rollers on the machine set fully apart, start feeding the dough into the machine. When the sheet comes out, lightly flour it, fold it over and put it through again. And again. Continue doing this a few times, until the sheet comes out feeling smooth and elastic. Again, flour it lightly and set it aside. Do the same with each remaining piece. This takes the place of your kneading.

Now, take each long, flat piece and, reducing the space between the rollers by one notch, put it through again.

Do this until you have narrowed the space between the rollers to the very minimum. After each sheet has been rolled out as thinly as the machine can roll it, set it aside and do the others. Then, when every sheet is rolled out long and flat, put each one through the cutting blades you've selected. Set the cut pasta aside to rest.

Pasta Fresca without Eggs

In this dough, water substitutes for the eggs. As before, mound up four cups of semolina (or regular "all-purpose" flour), make a deep well in the center and add one teaspoon of salt and one tablespoon of olive oil. Into this we want to incorporate about a cup of warm water. So, starting with about a quarter-cup, put the water into the well and mix the flour and water together with your fingertips. Continue to add more water to the center of the mound until you have incorporated all the water into the flour. If the mixture is getting too wet, stop there; if it's too dry after adding the cup of water, add more by teaspoons. Dough that is too wet is too sticky to work with; dough that is too dry breaks apart as you try to knead it or roll it out.

Set the dough aside in a ball to rest for 10 minutes; then proceed either by hand or by machine.

Cooking Pasta Fresca

Fresh pasta will cook up in a third the time, or less, of dried pasta. As with dried pasta, have plenty of water boiling strongly on the stove before you add the pasta. For a pound of pasta six quarts of water is minimum. (The more water you have at the boil the faster the pot will return to the boil after you put in your pasta, and the faster and better it all will cook.) Add a handful of salt; then stir in the pasta. You can also add a tablespoon or so of oil to keep the foaming to a minimum. Stir the pot from the bottom regularly to keep any pieces from sticking.

The pasta is done when it's still slightly firm and a bit chewy, but neither hard at the center, nor mushy altogether. Taste a piece every so often while it boils. And don't be intimidated by all those who say that pasta has to be drained at exactly the right moment of perfect al dentiness or it's ruined. There's a good and wide range between undercooked and too soft, so follow your own sense and taste.

As is true for both dry and fresh pasta, have a large, warm bowl with some of the sauce ready to receive the pasta as soon as it's drained. (And never, ever wash the pasta after it's been drained. Tap water adds nothing to the value of a bowl of pasta.) Put the pasta in the bowl, coat with the bit of sauce, then add the rest of the sauce and serve at once.

Pasta Names

I never spoke the word "pasta" until very late in my life. All "pasta" was either some variation of "spaghetti" or "macaroni." Spaghetti referred to anything long and thin — spaghetti, fettuccini, linguini, vermicelli ... Macaroni was anything otherwise; usually shaped and heavier — rotini, fusilli, manicotti tubes ... Ravioli, lasagna, and gnocchi were just called by their own names.

Whoever gave these pastas their names was an inventive genius, and a bit twisted at the edges. Spaghetti? No problem — strings. Manicotti? Muffs. Linguini? Small tongues. Ziti? Bridegrooms! Capellini? Little hairs. If you think it hard enough to sit down to eat a dish of something called little hairs, try a bowl of vermicelli — "little worms." And "pasta"? Sounds romantic, but it just means "paste." Sorry.

Caution

Having introduced you to the joys of fresh pasta, let me now add a cautionary note, one that may seem daunting but is actually meant to comfort: you will not get any of these recipes right the first time you try. You'll get something, and it will be good, but you will be frustrated and wish you had never even heard of pasta fresca. But the second time you do this, it will be easier. The third time, it'll be a breeze. Do not get discouraged.

Most of the sauces that follow can be used with either fresh or dried pasta.

Sauces

Tomato Sauce

I knew of no two Italian families that cooked tomato sauce the same way. Some swore by canned whole plum tomatoes; others began with garlic, olive oil, tomato paste, and water. Some started with crushed or pureed tomatoes; and, in the summer and fall, many families put together a sauce using fresh plum tomatoes and basil straight from the garden. There were those who added onions, some who diced in some carrots, and a few who even added a splash of red wine. Except on Fridays, there were usually some meatballs or sausages, or a nice piece of pork simmering along in the sauce.

Despite all these variations, I never knew anyone who used those thick concoctions that you simply needed to heat and pour over spaghetti. I never even knew anyone who had tried them, at least no Italians. It was almost a neighborhood taboo, like asking for a glass of buttermilk to have with fried squid. Rumor had it that prepared sauces were bought by the same people who served canned ravioli or who were tempted by those jars of soft Spaghetti-o's in that orange-colored sauce that smelled like warm catsup and made you wince.

Since those early, formative years I've managed to try a few of those already prepared sauces, and I have to report that the neighborhood prejudice was justified. Thick and sweet, they rarely taste anything like a good, homemade sauce. Often their second or third ingredient is corn syrup or sugar. There simply is no reason to buy these pre-made sauces. Tomato sauce is quite easy to make, it freezes well, it tastes delicious and it makes the whole house smell wonderful. You can vary it depending on your taste or the ingredients at hand. Once you've mastered it you will never again, even once, be tempted by ready-made sauces.

I generally think that the best kinds of canned tomatoes to buy are those that come labeled "ground" or "crushed." Not all brands carry tomatoes in this form, but they're worth looking for.

Using cans of ground or crushed tomatoes is something of an innovation — at least, we didn't often see them back when the Dodgers were still in town. But the result is usually superior to the next best alternative, which is buying cans of whole plum tomatoes, squeezing the seeds and the water out of each tomato, removing the small cores, chopping them, and cooking them in the garlic and oil.

All the recipes that follow use one 28 ounce (one pound, 12 ounce) can of tomatoes. When cooked, this is enough to sauce one pound of pasta, with a little left over to pass separately. One pound of pasta is usually enough to serve a family of four as a main course or six to eight as a first course. You can easily double or triple any of these tomato sauce recipes. And all these sauces will freeze quite well for months.

Tomato Sauce with Meat

Although the ingredients always can vary somewhat, the basic approach is generally the same. Brown some meat, then garlic, in a small amount of oil, add the tomatoes and herbs, and then cook slowly. For example:

In a tablespoon of oil in a large, heavy frying pan, brown one pound or more of meat. This can be whole Italian sausages (mild or hot), crumbled Italian sausage meat, a piece of lean pork, some cut-up spareribs, or a piece of beef. Over moderate heat, brown the meat well, but don't burn it. Remember, unlike French and Chinese cooking, almost all Italian foods are cooked over medium or low heat. If you're using whole sausages, puncture the skins in a few places with a sharp fork or knife-point to keep them from bursting.

While the meat is cooking, in a large saucepan gently brown one or two crushed garlic cloves in about two tablespoons of olive oil. (At this point some people add one small can of tomato paste and cook that, stirring, for about five minutes. Paste adds a little extra flavor and sweetness to the sauce and thickens it slightly. I generally don't think it's necessary.)

Add to the browned garlic one can of crushed or ground tomatoes and about a teaspoon of crushed oregano. Add about half a teaspoon of salt, and a few pinches of red pepper, if you'd like.

Remove the browned meat from the frying pan and add it to the sauce. Cover the pot, leaving a small space for steam to escape. If there were any browned meat bits in the bottom of the frying pan, pour off and discard the oil, add a quarter cup of water or a few scoops of the tomatoes that are cooking, and heat it all as you scrape the meat bits and browned juices from the bottom. Add this all to the sauce. If you have them, it's also traditional to add a few fresh basil leaves to the sauce while it simmers. (In truth, all the basil taste cooks away. But everyone did it anyway.)

Let this cook over very low heat for at least an hour, or until the meat is very tender and breaks apart with a fork. With a wooden spoon, stir it from the bottom thoroughly every few minutes. Please, under no circumstance allow the sauce to scorch.

Just before the pasta is done, remove the meat from the sauce. If you used pieces of pork or beef, slice them across the grain, about one-quarter inch thick. Put about half a cup or more of the sauce in the bottom of a large serving bowl. When the pasta is done, drain it well and add it to the sauce in the bowl. Stir it together to coat the pasta. Then add more of the sauce to the pasta in the bowl, gently lifting and stirring it all together. Arrange the meat on top, or, better still, serve it separately. Crushed red pepper and freshly grated Parmesan cheese can be passed at the table for those who would like some. Remember, one can of crushed tomatoes will cover one pound of pasta and serve four as a main course and up to eight as a first course.

As far as variations go, there are those who brown up a diced onion with the garlic, others who add sautéed sliced mushrooms or diced carrots to the sauce, and a small and unimpressive minority who add a diced celery stalk. I guess there's no harm in trying such things. But do remember that, in the end, the desired product is a relatively thick, richly flavored meat sauce, not a pot of hot V-8.

Not surprisingly, this basic recipe can be made "meatless" simply by not putting in any meat. This is what everyone back then simply called "marinara sauce" — I guess because it was assumed mariners, while they might have fish, would not have any meat with them. You may want to go slightly heavier on the garlic and herbs or toss in some fried mushrooms. Crushed red pepper, parmesan cheese, and much basil, all put over the hot and freshly sauced pasta finishes this dish just perfectly.

Tomato Sauce with Meatballs

Every Sunday — every Sunday — we ate meatballs. Meatballs and pasta. Sometimes we also had sausages, or a piece of pork, or a braciola in the sauce. But there were always meatballs, no matter what.

Cooking the meatballs is a three-step process: making them, frying them, finally cooking them in the tomato sauce. They make for a great tasting sauce, but my personal opinion is that they're best when just "fried," before you add them to the sauce. (I knew some people who formed the meatballs and put them, raw, into the tomato sauce and cooked them that way. For reasons easier sensed than explained, this is unspeakably barbaric.)

It's very easy to make a bad dish of spaghetti and meatballs, crude, tasteless, and tough. I've had it in restaurants where the meat tastes like anything but meat, soft, gray and packed with filler. So, rule number one: The meat should be left enough alone so that it tastes like meat. Rule number two: Don't squeeze the meat together so tightly that you could bounce it off the wall. With these few rules taken to heart, we can go on.

Start by putting together a batch of the sauce in the recipe for tomato sauce with meat (page 39). In this case, the meat will be these meatballs.

As the sauce simmers at the back of the stove, gently crumble two pounds of ground beef into a large bowl. I prefer ground chuck since I think it has the best ratio of lean to fat. (Ground pork can be added to the ground beef, even substituting for up to a third to a half the total weight.) Then take three or four slices of fresh or slightly stale white or Italian bread and crumble them into pieces about the size of your fingernail. Add them to the beef, mixing it gently with a fork. With every motion you want to open up the texture of the ground meat, not mash it. Add to this one scant tablespoon of dried oregano, a teaspoon of salt, a few grindings of black pepper, two cloves of crushed garlic, and a large handful of chopped Italian parsley. You can also add a few pinches of hot red pepper. (How much? Well, that should depend on how hot the pepper is, no?) If you have some fresh basil, add five or six chopped leaves. Mix all this in gently into the meat and bread.

In a separate bowl, scramble up two eggs with a teaspoon or so of water. With as light a touch as possible, stir this thoroughly into the meat mixture. With your fingertips, pick up the equivalent of one heaping tablespoon of meat and lightly form it into a ball in the cup of your hands. Compress each one just enough to hold together, no more. Remember, there is no prize for making the biggest meatballs in the neighborhood. In fact, you get demerits for that, and it goes on your permanent record. Make moderate sized meatballs, lightly formed. Two pounds of meat should give you about 20 meatballs.

Heat enough oil to cover lightly the bottom of a heavy frying pan. When the oil is hot, but before it starts to smoke, add enough meatballs to fit loosely in the pan. Reduce the heat to low and slowly fry the meatballs until they're richly brown on the outside – perhaps about 10 minutes or so. This is tricky, because you don't want them raw inside, yet you don't want them hard and overcooked either. (If you added ground pork to the mix, you may be more comfortable cooking each meatball till the center is more fully cooked.) So, when you think they're nearly done, break one open and look. If it's just right, eat it and put the others aside on a plate. If it's not cooked, cook it some more. Then eat it. Fry up the rest in the same way. (Do not, under any circumstances, resist the temptation to eat one or two right out of the frying pan. Plain, fried meatballs are one of life's great delights. Tell everyone you're just testing them to make sure they're done.)

Add the fried meatballs to the tomato sauce cooking at the back of the stove. Pour off all the oil remaining in the pan you fried the meatballs in and add some of the sauce to the hot pan. This is in order to pick up all the brown bits of meat still sticking to the pan. Stir this all around and add it back into the sauce.

There are a few possible variations to this recipe. You could, if you want, add three or four tablespoons of freshly grated Parmesan cheese to the meatballs as you mix them. I almost always do. Other herbs — fresh tarragon for example — could be lightly added, too. Under the heading of what not to do, there are those who add pine nuts or raisins, or both, to their meatballs. This is one of the things that gave Sicilians a bad reputation.

Tomato Sauce with Braciole

In Brooklyn-Italian a braciola is a large, flat piece of beef covered with a bread stuffing, then rolled, tied, and simmered in tomato sauce. Even though it sounds interesting, it's not particularly "company food," although we used to add them to the sauce with meatballs, spareribs, and sausages for when the whole family got together.

First, however, an Italian lesson: One braciola is just that, a braciola. Two or more braciole are, well, braciole. But both are pronounced, badly, the same way — brazhol'. Crazy what Brooklyn can do to the world's most lyrical language!

To make braciole, take four pieces of very thinly cut top or bottom round steak and dry them on paper towels. (They should be no more than a quarter-inch thick — thinner, if possible.) In a bowl mix one cup breadcrumbs, a quarter cup grated Parmesan cheese, one crushed clove of garlic, a half cup of chopped parsley, one teaspoon crushed dried oregano, and either a heaping tablespoon of basil leaves or a half-tablespoon chopped fresh rosemary leaves. To give the filling a fine taste and keep it moist, fry up a chopped onion in some oil and add that to the bread as well. (There were always some families who would also add a handful of raisins.) In a separate bowl, beat one egg with a teaspoon of water and add that to the breadcrumb mixture. Stir it all together well.

Lay the meat out flat and fill up the center of each with a quarter of the moistened bread mixture, leaving the outer quarter inch or so uncovered all around. Roll each one up like a jelly-roll. Now take about two feet of kitchen string for each braciola and tie each one up so that it will keep its shape as it cooks. (Actually, we always tied them up with sewing thread, which was generally impossible to find once the meat was cooked, and we splattered sauce all over everything when we tried to break the thread away at the table. Kitchen twine is a great improvement.)

Fry the meat rolls in a quarter-cup oil (olive oil is unnecessary here) in a heavy frying pan over medium heat. When the rolls are browned on all sides, pour off the oil. Add two large (28 oz.) cans of crushed tomatoes and simmer, partly covered, for two hours.

Before serving, remove the meat from the sauce, discard the strings, cut each braciola into slices about a half-inch thick, and pass the meat separately.

This sauce goes well with most pasta, especially heavier macaroni, such as ziti, fusilli, or rigatoni. And don't forget that different varieties of sauce-meat — sausage, braciole, spareribs, meatballs, and pieces of beef or pork — can all be cooked and served together.

Tomato Sauce with Ground Beef

This is the simplest and easiest way to make a tomato sauce with meat. Just crumble up a half pound or pound of ground beef (or a mixture of ground beef, pork, and veal) and fry it up in some olive oil with a crushed clove or two of garlic. Drain off any excess oil and fat, add a can or two of crushed tomatoes, and cook as you would for sauce with meat. There are some baked pasta dishes, such as cannelloni, lasagna, or manicotti, where this kind of sauce seems just right.

Tomato Sauce with Fresh Tomatoes

This is a sauce that should keep its fresh, light taste. It should be cooked just enough to get out the excess water.

In a large pot of boiling water, plunge 10 or 12 fully ripe Italian plum tomatoes. Remove them 30 seconds after the water returns to the simmer and run them under cold water. Peel, core, and gently squeeze each one to press out the seeds and as much water as will come. Chop them roughly and set them aside.

Fry a clove of garlic, chopped or crushed, in three tablespoons of olive oil. When just golden, add the tomato pulp and stir, over high heat, until much of the water has cooked off. Turn the heat down to low and add a pinch or two of salt. Simmer this uncovered, stirring often, for about 10 minutes. Add a scant handful of chopped basil leaves and simmer it all for another minute. To serve, simply mix the sauce into a bowl of cooked pasta, sprinkle with chopped parsley (or chopped parsley and basil mixed) and serve.

For variety, try flavoring the tomatoes and basil with a quarter pound of prosciutto or pancetta instead of the garlic. Simply cut the meat into thin strips and heat it in the oil for a few seconds before you add the tomatoes. You can also add an onion or carrot, both very finely chopped. Or you could add a teaspoon of lightly crushed anise or fennel seeds when you put in the salt, especially if you don't have any basil.

These sauces go well with any kind of pasta, from the thinnest and most delicate to heavy dishes like gnocchi. They may be at their very best not with store-bought pastas but with your own, fresh and homemade.

Red Clam Sauce

If you love the taste of clams, then you should probably avoid smothering them with too much tomato or any heavy sauce. Here's a good way to do it where the taste of tomato complements and carries, rather than suffocates, the taste of the clams. This will feed four as a first course. Increase all ingredients proportionally to feed more.

In summer, buy half a dozen or so perfectly ripe Italian plum tomatoes. Peel them by dropping them in boiling water for about 30 seconds. Then run them under cold water. When you can handle them, peel them, remove their cores, squeeze out some of the water, and chop them roughly. If you don't have fresh tomatoes buy a can of whole tomatoes, drain them, remove their cores, squeeze them gently to remove the seeds and excess water, and chop them.

In a deep saucepan, slowly heat a quarter cup of olive oil with two crushed cloves of garlic. As soon as the garlic begins to color, add the tomatoes with a half teaspoon of salt and cook this, covered, over low heat, while you prepare the clams. If at any time it looks like the tomatoes will burn, add a few tablespoons of water.

Buy about two dozen small, hardshell, littleneck clams and four or five larger "cherrystones." These larger clams are necessary since the smaller ones often have too little juice to make a sauce. Scrub all of them thoroughly in cool water. Discard any that are open. In another saucepan with another quarter-cup of olive oil add all the well-scrubbed clams, cover, and, over medium-high heat, cook the clams until they open. With tongs, remove the clams to a bowl as they open, continuing to cook those that are still closed. After about five minutes of cooking and shaking the pan, discard any that refuse to open. You should now have at least a good half-cup of juice in the pan. If not, you'll have to add a bit of water to make it up.

Now, pour the clam broth through a strainer (to remove any bit of sand) into the simmering tomato and leave it on very low heat to simmer. Remove the meat from the larger clams, chop it roughly, and add to the tomato-clam juice mix to simmer. (You still have the two dozen or so smaller clams, cooked and open in their shells, in another bowl.)

Now, in a pot of rapidly boiling water, put a scant tablespoon of salt and about a pound of spaghettini, thin linguini, or capellini. With this sauce, thinner spaghetti works best. As the pasta cooks, put a few tablespoons of the hot clam sauce into a large, heated bowl. When the pasta is done, drain it well and mix it with the sauce in the bowl. Add the open clams sitting in the bowl to the remainder of the sauce, heat them very quickly, and pour it all, sauce and clams, over the pasta. Toss it well with a tablespoon or two of fresh-snipped basil or a handful of chopped parsley and serve.

Tomato Sauce with Mussels

There are two ways to do this, one with the mussels cooked directly in the tomato sauce, one not.

The first way is to make a very plain meatless tomato sauce (as written above, page 37). While the sauce is simmering slowly, scrub about two dozen mussels and debeard them. (See, above, page 28). Any mussels that are open and will not close when you tap them should not be used. Now, some mussels will not have beards. As you scrub these, move the shells back and forth a bit to be certain there's a live mussel in there holding tightly onto its shell and not just two shells with mud inside. As you might guess, the last thing you want is tomato sauce with mud.

After the sauce has simmered slowly for about an hour and thickened somewhat, add the scrubbed, debearded mussels. (If they were closed tightly when you cleaned them and only started to open after you debearded them, that's fine. Keep them cool and use them within the hour you cleaned them and they're OK.) Simmer the mussels slowly for about five minutes or until they're all open. Try not to overcook them. Remove the mussels, mix the sauce with a pound of linguini, cooked al dente, and put the mussels, still in their shells, over the top. Chop a handful of parsley and put that over the top as well. Serve at once.

It has always seemed to me that a platter of linguini, with the red of the sauce, the blackness of the mussels, the creamy-white of the pasta and the green of the parsley, has to be one of the most beautiful sights in all of cooking.

The second way is slightly more complex: Begin the tomato sauce as above. In another saucepan heat a few tablespoons of olive oil, a crushed clove of garlic, a finely minced very small onion or a few minced scallions, and either a teaspoon of lightly crushed anise seed or a teaspoon of dried tarragon. Heat this very slowly until the garlic begins to turn golden. Now add the cleaned, debearded mussels. Shake them back and forth in the pan until they're all open. Set the mussels aside, covered.

Now, gently boil the broth the mussels have left behind in the pan for about a minute to reduce it slightly; then strain it into the simmering tomato sauce. Cook the sauce for about a half-hour altogether. Then add the mussels, still in their shells, to the sauce to warm them through. Pour the sauce and mussels over the top of the cooked spaghetti or linguini and sprinkle with chopped parsley.

Be forewarned: Since these sauces are thinner than most and since trying to get each mussel out of its shell isn't always as easy as it seems, you will get spots on your white shirt and you will get spots on your dress. One partial solution is to tuck your napkin under your chin, where I always thought it belonged anyway. Another is to take the mussels out of their shells in the kitchen and put them on top of the pasta naked. (Since the black shells are beautiful, you can arrange them around the sides of the platter for decoration.) But these are only partial solutions. Don't eat pasta with mussels before you go to the opera because you will get a spot on your tux sleeve no matter how hard you try not to.

Tomato Sauce with Crabs

There is also more than one way to make crab sauce. The way my grandmother used to do it is she'd get a great big pot of tomato sauce bubbling on the stove; then she'd add a half-dozen large live crabs, let them cook for half an hour, then pour it all over spaghetti. It actually tastes great, but it's not the most appetizing sight around. Besides, the sauce tends to be so thin that when you try to crack the crab shells at the table, you not only get it on your shirt, you get it on the wallpaper.

A second way is slightly more difficult but considerably more presentable: Start the basic tomato sauce described above in the recipe for sauce with mussels. While that's simmering very quietly towards the back of the stove, in a large pot steam six good-sized crabs. Do not boil them – steam them, covered with a lid, in about two inches of water. They're done when their shells turn a bright orange-red, in about 15 to 20 minutes. Discard the cooking water and let the crabs cool until they can be easily handled. Crack the crabs over a bowl to catch all the liquid that comes out. Remove as much crabmeat as you can, putting the meat in a separate bowl. Strain the crab liquid into the simmering tomato sauce and let it cook another 15 minutes. Add the crabmeat, immediately turn off the heat, and serve it over pasta. As usual, sprinkle with chopped parsley.

The third way to make a sauce of tomatoes with crab is not to use canned tomatoes but to make a sauce with fresh tomatoes that we saw a few pages back, leaving out the garlic. Then — and here's the most beautiful part — don't buy fresh crabs, buy a pound of mixed backfin and claw crabmeat instead! Add the crabmeat to a quarter cup of very good olive oil in which you've lightly browned a small clove (no more) of minced or crushed garlic and perhaps a minced shallot or a few minced scallions and heat the crabmeat thoroughly in the oil/garlic/shallot mixture. Once the crab has sautéed for a minute in the oil, pour it all into the fresh tomato sauce you began a short while before. Add a small handful of chopped basil, or basil and parsley, and pour it all over a cooked pound of angel hair pasta, capellini, or thin spaghetti. No fuss, no steaming the crabs and picking the meat from the shells, no big kitchen mess …

This is best eaten outdoors, on a breezy summer's day, as a first course, with good friends and a bottle of white wine. Resist the temptation to eat it all by yourself in the kitchen.

Tripe and Sauce

Tripe causes fights. There are those, myself included, who love it with a passion that surpasseth all understanding. Others would sooner eat mice. I will give you the best tripe recipe I know.

Peel four good-sized onions. Cut them in half lengthwise; then cut each half into slices a quarter-inch thick. Mince or crush four cloves of garlic. Add the onions and garlic to a quarter-cup olive oil in a large pan that can go in the oven. Set the heat at 350° and cook the onions in the oven, covered, for about 40 minutes, or until they're golden. Stir them two or three times as they cook.

While the onions are cooking, wash two pounds of tripe under cold, running water. Then place it in a large pot of simmering salted water. Slowly simmer the tripe for about five minutes; then drain it and wash it again in cold water. If you think you might want to lighten the taste of the tripe more, simmer it in the same manner once again. But, please, try not to let the tripe boil, or it will toughen and take longer to cook correctly.

Now, with a sharp knife, cut the tripe into squares an inch to an inch-and-a-half on each side, discarding any visible fat. When the onions are golden, lower the heat to 300°, and add the drained tripe with about a teaspoon of salt. Also add the following, either in one of these handy aluminum tea balls or tied in a square of washed cheesecloth: a dozen peppercorns, a bay leaf, six dried allspice berries or four cloves, and a teaspoon of fennel or anise seeds. Add a few sprigs of Italian parsley directly into the tripe. Often, I'll use a potato peeler to cut two or three strips of orange peel or tangerine peel from the very outside skin of the fruit and add that to the seasoning as well. Let this all cook in the oven, covered, for about one hour. The tripe and onions should give off water as they cook. Check after 20 or 30 minutes, and, if it all seems dry and the tripe is sticking to the pan, add a half cup of chicken stock or chicken stock and white wine mixed.

At the end of the hour add five or six plum tomatoes, either canned or fresh, to the tripe. If you're using fresh tomatoes you'll have to peel them. (As always, the easiest way to do this is to put them in a large pot of rapidly boiling water for about 30 seconds, then drain them. They should now peel fairly easily.) Whether canned or fresh, remove the core and squeeze out the seeds and much of the water. Chop them coarsely and add them to the slowly bubbling tripe and onions. Cook it for another two hours.

The tripe should be simmering in a good bit of liquid. If it's not, add more chicken stock or stock and wine. When done there should be at least a cup of liquid. Remove the pack of spices, the parsley sprigs and any peel before you serve it.

Cooked in this manner the tripe can be eaten simply as a main course, with some bread and a salad, or it can be used as a sauce for pasta. It goes excellently with all pastas except the most delicate. Try it with spaghetti or fettuccelle, or with a heavier macaroni such as fusili or rotelle (spirals). Sprinkle the pasta with chopped parsley before serving and pass a dish of grated Parmesan for anyone who'd like it. With a pound of pasta, the recipe will easily feed six or eight. Without pasta, it will feed four.

Tripe in Tomato Sauce

This is what is known in the Old Country simply as Trippa a la Romana.

After parboiling – actually "parsimmering" would be more correct to say – one pound of tripe as described in the recipe above, cut the tripe into one inch squares, or strips one inch by one-and-a-half inches. Then, in a large saucepan, sauté the tripe very slowly in one-quarter cup olive oil for about 15 minutes. Add two crushed cloves of garlic and again sauté, slowly, for another five minutes. The tripe will release some liquid but try not to let it come to a boil or it will toughen and the final cooking will take that much longer.

In a large square of washed cheesecloth, put one-eighth of a teaspoon of crushed red pepper, one teaspoon anise or fennel seeds, a half teaspoon of oregano, two sprigs parsley and a bay leaf. Secure this mix tightly and bury it in the tripe. Add salt, pepper and one large (28 oz.) can of crushed tomatoes. Cover and simmer it all very slowly for three to four hours. If the sauce gets too thick, do not hesitate to add some water, chicken stock, or beef stock.

Pour this sauce over any heavy pasta and serve each bowl with a good handful of grated Parmesan cheese.

Baked Pasta with Tomato Sauces

Lasagna

Good lasagna is simply delicious. Even bad lasagna isn't half bad.

It takes all of a Sunday morning to make lasagna. Happily, this is one of those few dishes that you'll have around longer than it takes to make. And (up to a point) it actually gets better as it sits.

First, prepare a quart of richly flavored tomato sauce with meat. If you have a quart in the freezer, defrost it, heat it gently till warm, and set the meat aside. Set your oven at 325°.

Second, in a large pot of rapidly boiling salted water, cook one pound of lasagna noodles. It might help to add a few spoonfuls of oil – not to keep the noodles from sticking, as most cookbooks declare, but to help keep the foam from boiling over onto the stove. To reduce sticking, add the noodles one or two at a time. Cook until each noodle is al dente – just done, with the slightest resistance when you bite a piece. Drain the noodles thoroughly in a colander. If you want to use homemade noodles, by all means do so. Simply cut the rolled strips about 10 inches long by three inches wide and boil them for about six minutes in salted water. Drain in a colander and proceed.

Third, take two pounds of whole milk ricotta cheese and add salt and pepper to taste. Taste for saltiness. Now, beat into the ricotta one or two eggs. (Ever since I read in an old farmhouse cookbook a recipe for eggnog that said, "If the hen was sick, your guests will die," I have always tasted everything before I add the raw egg.)

Fourth, grate one cup or more of Parmesan cheese. Please, do not use pre-packaged grated cheese.

Fifth, chop about a cup of Italian parsley leaves.

Sixth, thinly slice one pound of the freshest mozzarella you can buy and put the slices on a paper towel to dry.

Seventh, snip or chop about a quarter cup of fresh basil leaves.

(I've set it out this way, in seven steps, since this actually tracks the order of construction.)

Now take a baking pan about 8" by 12". Spoon enough tomato sauce onto the pan to lightly film the bottom. Cover the sauce with as many noodles as needed to fit the bottom of the pan. Although perfection is not required, if they overlap too much, cut them each to fit.

On top of the noodles, spread a few spoonfuls of the ricotta-egg mixture as well as some of the grated Parmesan. Put about a third of the chopped parsley over it and then lay a few slices of the mozzarella on top of that.

Spoon some tomato sauce over this, put about a third of the basil on the sauce, and top it all with another layer of noodles. You now have one complete layer — noodles, ricotta/egg, Parmesan, parsley, mozzarella, tomato sauce, basil, and noodles once again. Repeat until all the ingredients are finished, ending with the last few noodles, a wash of sauce, and a few pieces of mozzarella on top.

Don't worry if there are gaps or overlaps, or if some layers seem fuller than others. Believe me, it will all taste just fine.

Now, put the lasagna in an oven (preheated to 325°) and let it cook slowly for about 45 minutes to an hour. (You might want to cover the pan with foil for the first half of the cooking, then uncovering it so the top might brown ever so slightly.) Remove from the oven and let the lasagna sit for at least a half hour before you serve it.

How to serve it? Well, it can be the main course of a meal, perhaps with a salad and some of the pork or ribs or sausage that cooked in the tomato sauce. On festive days you can serve small squares of it as a first course, before the roast or the turkey. And don't forget to heat some up in the oven for lunch the next day. You'll find that it's even better then, when all the tastes have melded together.

Baked Ziti

I always thought of baked ziti as the lazy man's lasagna, though in truth it's almost as much work. But instead of using lasagna noodles, you need to boil up a pound of ziti — short, hollow pasta tubes.

Before you begin this recipe, make or defrost at least four cups of tomato sauce with ground beef, or tomato sauce with cooked mild Italian sausage crumbled in. (You don't need a recipe for this — just fry up some crumbled homemade Italian sausage meat, add two cans of crushed tomatoes, and cook till it's done.) As I say, have this heating on the back of the stove before you begin the ziti.

Now bring a very large pot of salted water to the boil and add a box of ziti. While the ziti are boiling, mix two pounds of whole milk ricotta cheese, a handful or two of chopped Italian parsley, a cup of grated fresh Parmesan cheese (or half cup of Parmesan and half cup of Romano), a full cup of shredded fresh mozzarella cheese, plus salt and pepper to taste. Grating a bit of nutmeg into the cheese mixture is not uncommon and adds a nice flavor. (Interestingly, basil tends to be the flavoring added to lasagna, and nutmeg to ziti, though I'm sure you could do it the other way around. If you do, the only thing that will suffer is Tradition.) Unlike the lasagna, which you want to become somewhat firm, baked ziti is always looser in texture, so leave off mixing in any eggs.

When the ziti are done, remove from the heat and drain very, very well. Remember, a lot of water can hide in those hollow tubes, so shake the colander strongly.

In a 12" by 8" baking pan or something near thereto, put a thin base of the tomato sauce. In a bowl add a few ladles of the sauce to the drained ziti – enough so that the ziti are coated with sauce but not swimming in it. Put a heavy layer of this sauced ziti in the bottom of the baking pan, add half the ricotta cheese mixture, a few spoonfuls more of sauce, the rest of the coated ziti, and end with the remainder of the cheese mixture. If you want, you can put some sauce over the top. Bake it all in a 350 – 375° oven for about half an hour. Since baked ziti is much looser than lasagna, you'll need to spoon it out rather than try to cut it into neat squares. Pass around extra grated Parmesan and the remainder of the tomato sauce and serve with a green salad and more than a few glasses of red wine.

Like lasagna, this is even better the next day.

Manicotti

Baked manicotti is prepared very much like lasagna or ziti, except that, like ravioli, the cheese, egg, and parsley mix is stuffed into the shells rather than layered separately with sauce.

Here's what to do – In boiling salted water cook a dozen or more manicotti tubes for six to eight minutes. When just barely done — still somewhat firm to the bite — remove them to a colander and drain completely. Take all the ingredients for lasagna — ricotta, Parmesan, mozzarella (cubed, not sliced), egg, parsley, basil, salt and pepper — and, using a spoon, fill each tube generously with this mixture. Place the manicotti in a baking dish whose bottom is coated with a generous amount of tomato sauce. The dish should be just large enough to hold them all in one compact layer. Pour more sauce over and around the manicotti and generously cover the top with shredded mozzarella or grated Parmesan, or both. Bake in a pre-heated 325° oven for about 30 minutes, or until the cheese on to begins to color and the sauce is bubbling gently here and there.

Stuffed shells can be prepared in exactly the same way.

Cannelloni

Cannelloni come in a number of forms. You can sometimes buy dried pasta cannelloni tubes, not unlike manicotti. You can make extra-thin fresh pasta sheets, boil them quickly, and roll them around the cannelloni filling. Or you can make a kind of crepe from flour, eggs, and water and use that as the "tube" for a ricotta filling. You can bake your cannelloni with either a tomato or béchamel sauce. Here's how to do it with tomato sauce and crepes:

First, it helps if you have a rich tomato sauce already made. As with most baked pastas, my favorite is one with ground meat — ground beef or crumpled Italian sausage meat — cooked directly into the sauce (see page 37), though a sauce with a piece of pork or a braciola served with the cannelloni makes for a fuller meal.

For the crepes, beat three eggs with one cup of water. Add one cup of all-purpose flour, scooped from the bag and scraped level with the back of a knife. Whisk this all together. The mixture should have the consistency of thin pancake batter. If too thin, add more flour. If too thick, add more water. Heat an 8" frying pan with sloping sides over medium-high heat until a drop of water "dances" on the surface. If the pan is well seasoned, add some oil or butter and quickly wipe it out. If the pan is not seasoned, film it very lightly with some oil.

Add a scant quarter-cup of batter to the pan and rotate the pan so that the batter covers the bottom. Don't worry too much about holes or bare spots. (You want the batter to thinly cover the bottom of the pan.) In a few seconds, the bottom of the crepe will be lightly browned. With a fork, flip it over for a few more seconds, then remove it to a towel or paper towel to cool. Make the rest of the crepes the same way, adding them to the towel as you go. It's OK to pile them up. You should get 12 to 15 crepes altogether.

For the filling, thoroughly mix a small container of fresh ricotta cheese (usually about 15 oz.) with two eggs. Add about a quarter pound of fresh mozzarella cheese, thinly sliced and chopped, a large handful of chopped Italian parsley leaves, a quarter-cup (more or less) of grated

Parmesan cheese, and salt and pepper to taste. If you'd like, a few snips of basil leaf can go in as well.

Take a baking pan large enough to hold all the crepes in one layer and heavily coat the bottom with tomato sauce. (Or have two pans, each one holding half the cannelloni.) Lay one crepe on the counter, browner side down. Put about two tablespoons of filling near one edge of the crepe and roll it up so you have something that looks like a medium sized cigar, open at both ends. If it looks too skinny, you should have put in more filling. Open it up, add more, then re-roll. (You should have more than enough filling for a dozen crepes.) Place it in the pan with the tomato sauce. Keep going until you've filled all the crepes.

Spoon some tomato sauce over the top and sides of the crepes, add some shredded mozzarella, cover with foil, and bake in a preheated 325° oven until the sauce starts to bubble around the sides. Take it out, let it cool a bit (so the filling "sets") and serve it with the rest of the tomato sauce, piping hot.

Two cannelloni make a wonderful first course. Three or more, with a salad, make a fine supper – especially with some of the sauce meat on the side.

Other Pastas

Ravioli

Although there are several varieties of authentic Italian ravioli — meat filled, cheese filled, even filled with pumpkin — the one probably most familiar to Italian-Americans is the one made with cheese and served with tomato sauce. And, while frozen, store-bought ravioli are OK, they're simply not as good as homemade. Besides, making ravioli from scratch is fun.

We can begin with the same ingredients we used for fresh pasta with egg, though we needn't make as much. So, prepare a dough using two cups semolina flour, two eggs, two teaspoons of olive oil, about a half-teaspoon of salt, and four to six tablespoons of warm water. You can mix it, knead it, and roll it out by hand, as on page 32; or you can use the pasta machine. In any event, you want to start with long, flat, very thin strips of dough.

(Our aim is to put a few dollops of filling on each strip of dough, cover it with a another, seal each mound of filling all around, and then cut each mound into something that looks like a little pillow square. You know.)

Once you've rolled out your long strips of very thin dough, whether by hand or by machine, set them aside, separated, and covered with a kitchen towel, and prepare the filling.

In a bowl mix a container of fresh ricotta cheese (about a pound) with a half-cup of freshly grated Parmesan and a half pound of fresh mozzarella cheese, cut into small dice and thoroughly dried. If the ricotta seems very wet, put it in a large sieve over a bowl and let it drain. Whip together one egg with the yolks of two others, and mix that thoroughly into the cheese filling. Season with salt (perhaps a half-teaspoon or more) and freshly ground black pepper. Add a good handful of chopped Italian parsley leaves.

Lay one strip of dough out flat on a countertop. If the dough is at all sticky, lightly dust the counter with flour. Drop a rounded teaspoon of filling every inch and a half or so on the strip. With your finger (or a small brush) paint a line of cold water around each dollop of filling. Lay another sheet of dough lightly on top of the bottom sheet and press firmly along the water lines you just painted so that the top sheet sticks tightly to the bottom. With either a knife or (better) a serrated pastry wheel, cut between each "pillow" and place them in one layer on a lightly floured cookie sheet to dry slightly. Repeat until you run out of dough or filling or cookie sheets or patience.

To cook, slide each ravioli into a very large pot of simmering salted water, and continue to simmer them slowly for approximately eight to ten minutes. After about six minutes, take one out and test for doneness. Ravioli are one of the few pastas that can't take turbulent boiling. Keep the pot at a very slow simmer, lest the ravioli break apart.

Gently spoon the ravioli into a colander and let them drain thoroughly. Have whatever sauce you've prepared ready when the ravioli are done; then put them in a large, heated bowl, cover gently with sauce, and serve. Freshly grated Parmesan can be passed at the table.

Spinach and Cheese Filling for Ravioli

This makes a good substitute for the plainer all cheese filling. It is equally good in either ravioli or cannelloni.

Thoroughly wash, stem, cook, and chop a large bunch of spinach leaves, enough to give you at least a half cup of cooked spinach when done. Simmer the leaves in a few cups of water for about four minutes, or until tender. Drain the leaves well, chop very fine, and squeeze them as dry as you can. In a large bowl combine the spinach with a 15 oz. container of whole-milk ricotta cheese, one whole egg plus two egg yolks, a scant quarter-cup of grated Parmesan, a half pound of diced mozzarella, a teaspoon of salt, and a few grindings of black pepper. You may want to add the tiniest grating of nutmeg as well.

Use this exactly as you would the regular cheese filling.

Gnocchi

Gnocchi are, in a way, a sort of cross between pasta fresca and dumplings. The trick is to keep them as light as possible.

Potato Gnocchi

This recipe might seem odd, since it calls for boiling baking potatoes (such as russets) rather than using ordinary boiling potatoes. But the mealiness of baking potatoes is exactly what's needed to keep the gnocchi light. This recipe will make enough gnocchi to feed four for dinner.

Peel two pounds (about three russets) of baking potatoes and cut into quarters — or smaller if the potatoes are very large. Put them into a large pot of rapidly boiling salted water, lower the heat to medium as it returns to a boil and cook, covered, until tender, perhaps 20 minutes. You want the potatoes to be cooked through but not falling apart.

When done, thoroughly drain the potatoes in a colander. You can even return them to the empty pot over medium heat to evaporate any excess moisture. Be careful that they don't scorch.

If you have a potato ricer or one of those old-fashioned chinoise with the tapered wooden pestles, now's the time to use it. They work well at keeping the potatoes light. Otherwise, mash the potatoes with a regular potato masher or even with a sturdy fork. In a large bowl combine the riced or mashed potatoes with a teaspoon of salt, some pepper, and two cups of regular, all-purpose flour. Mix thoroughly, then make a well in the center and add two whole eggs and four egg yolks, thoroughly beaten. With your fingers or a strong wooden spoon, turn this into a dough. It should be somewhat sticky.

Now spread a few handfuls of flour on a spotlessly clean countertop. Take a handful of the potato-egg-flour dough and roll it back and forth in the flour with the palms of your hands until you have a "rope" about two-thirds of an inch thick. Set it aside and continue rope making until all the dough is used up. Cut the ropes into one-inch-long pieces. It's traditional to put some sort of mark or indentation into each gnocchi, I imagine better to capture sauce. You can easily do this by pressing the back of the tines of a fork onto each piece, though it's perfectly fine just to leave the gnocchi alone.

To cook, bring a large pot of salted water to a boil and drop in about a dozen gnocchi at a time. They will sink at first, then float. Let them cook for only three or four minutes after they rise; then remove them with a slotted spoon and drain them a little longer in a bowl lined with paper towels. Continue with the rest of the gnocchi until all are done. Put them in a heated bowl with a little sauce, coating them thoroughly and adding more sauce as necessary.

But what kind of sauce? Any kind of tomato sauce goes well with gnocchi, from a heavy meat sauce to a light fresh sauce with plenty of basil. And pesto is simply wonderful. But my favorite sauce these days is one that was never found in our neighborhood, although it's quite traditional in parts of Italy. Simply heat two sticks of butter over a medium flame with a dozen fresh sage leaves until the butter starts to brown. Add half a cup of shelled walnut halves and heat through. Toss with the gnocchi in a warmed bowl and serve. You can also add grated Parmesan if you'd like.

Spinach Gnocchi

The simplest way to make spinach gnocchi is to follow the recipe above for potato gnocchi, reducing the number of eggs to one whole egg and three yolks and adding a quarter cup of Parmesan cheese and a quarter-cup of finely chopped cooked spinach, either fresh or frozen. Make sure the spinach is squeezed very dry. Cut, cook, and sauce as above.

Pastina

Pastina — tiny pasta stars— is Italian comfort food. It's also one of the few foods that my mother would put butter on. Cooking it is simplicity itself.

Into four to six quarts of boiling salted water stir a pound of pastina. (This will be more than enough for a hearty lunch for four.) Since pastina tends to foam up more than most pastas, you should add a teaspoon or so of oil to the water. Cook for a few minutes, tasting every now and then. Pastina cooks quickly, so be careful.

When done, drain it thoroughly and put it into a warm bowl with a half-stick of butter. Stir in a half-cup or more of Parmesan cheese, just grated, mix and sprinkle with a handful of chopped parsley. Salt and pepper to taste. That's it.

Well, that's it, unless you want to vary it. You could use a half-cup of excellent, fruity olive oil instead of the butter. You could add a half-cup of warmed cream or mascarpone cheese to the pastina before adding the parsley. (Mom would hate it but it's excellent.) Or you could add a quarter pound of hard salami, cut into thin slivers, or a quarter pound of not-too-thinly sliced prosciutto ham, also cut into slivers. The more you add, the richer and more festive the dish becomes. But don't slight just plain pastina with butter, salt, and pepper. It's just plain wonderful.

A Note on Cheeses

There are five cheeses produced in Italy that are world-class: Parmesan, Gorgonzola, ricotta, mozzarella, and mascarpone. Two of these — ricotta and mozzarella — are now produced fresh in America and are virtually as good as the originals. (I do believe that mozzarella made in Italy with buffalo milk is spectacular, with a richer and somewhat tangier taste than its American counterpart. But in most dishes where the mozzarella is combined with other ingredients, such as pastas and sauces, it simply isn't worth the extra price of import.) Parmesan is now made everywhere from here in the U.S. to Argentina, but none compares to the original, from Parma. True Parmesan — Parmigiano-Reggiano — is absolutely and unquestionably worth the price. It may simply be the world's best cheese.

Gorgonzola, like its saltier French counterpart Roquefort, is excellent in small pieces as a desert cheese with fruit and in some salads. And mascarpone is what angels eat on feast days. (I've taken to using it not only in such dishes as pastina with thin slivers of meat, but on my morning English muffin with marmalade — proving, once again, that this is not a "diet" book.)

Now here's where I get into trouble. There are Italian cheeses I do not like. At the top of the list is Provolone. Chunks of it are traditional in antipasto, and pieces of it might be eaten as a between-meal snack. I find that it is often so sharp that it causes welts in my mouth. No thanks. And Romano, Asiago and Locatelli are often too salty, less complex, and simply not as nutty and sweetly interesting as good Parmesan.

A Note on Olive Oils

Having made an admission on cheeses, it's now time to make a confession on olive oils. Not all olive oil is the same, and I don't just mean the difference between "pure" and "extra virgin." In the old days, we actually used oil that was, bluntly, diluted olive oil. The large cans labeled "olive oil" that grandma poured from were, if memory serves me right, only 15% olive. The rest was probably canola oil or some similar bland ingredient. Only now, with greater affluence, do we buy oils that are 100% olive.

Perhaps because of what I had as a child, I still prefer lighter olive oils to heavier ones. This distinction between lighter (and at their best "fruity") and heavier (sometimes even "peppery") oils can often cut across the "pure" versus "extra virgin" distinction. Experiment and see what fits your taste. But don't automatically think that because it costs more you'll like it better. You might not.

I now keep a few different olive oils on hand. I use an inexpensive, often "pure" one for general frying and a very expensive, but very light and fruity, almost flowery, one for dishes where the taste of the oil is prominent. But I'll use a heavier, more peppery oil in some things, like salads with vinegar, where the taste of the oil is mixed and blended with other flavors. I even have a strong but smooth and un-peppery olive oil from Morocco that tastes exactly like cured black olives and is wonderful for dipping bread into but whose taste completely evaporates if you try to use it for cooking.

By the way, the distinction between "pure" and "extra virgin" refers to different modes of processing, with "extra virgin" referring to oil from the first, often cold, pressing of the olives. "Pure" refers to oil from olives that have been previously pressed but are later mixed with water, heated, and from which more oil is then mechanically separated. Inexplicably, when it comes to olive oils, there seem to be almost no plain "virgins" ever sent our way.

Pasta Sauces with Olive Oil

Aglio e Olio

Literally, garlic and oil — and that's pretty much all it is.

I was tempted to write that this is the lunch to make when the fridge is empty or you're in a rush or you've just gone broke, but that would make it seem like something you'd only make under duress. It's far, far from that. There are some afternoons when a big bowl of aglio e olio is the most satisfying meal you can make.

In boiling, salted water, cook linguini al dente. Again, a pound will feed four happily for lunch. (This recipe covers a pound.) While it's boiling, chop some Italian, flat-leaf parsley (maybe two handfuls), and set aside. Slowly heat a half-cup of your favorite olive oil with three or four thinly sliced garlic cloves. Sauté the garlic over such low heat that it softens and ever so slightly takes on a golden color, but under no circumstances allow it to burn. When the garlic is just about ready, add two or three good pinches of red pepper flakes, or to taste, and remove it from the heat.

When the pasta is just cooked, fork it out of the pot and into a large bowl. Your aim is to have a good bit of the water the pasta was cooked in cling to the strands. Pour the oil-garlic-pepper sauce over the noodles, add salt to taste, and serve.

You could also mash three or four anchovy fillets into the garlic and oil as it cooks. With or without the anchovies, you also could add about a half-cup of grated Parmesan cheese as well.

A Note on Simplicity of Taste

Those of you who are good cooks and grew up in America after the wonderful revolution in cooking that started almost 60 years ago might be surprised at the simplicity and even starkness of so many of these recipes. Oil and garlic on pasta ... tomatoes, mozzarella, and basil ... chicken broth with escarole ... Over the years we've turned to thinking that the art of cooking is the art of being fancy. Much French cooking, for example, is highly composed, with a wealth of ingredients in each dish, all blending together to form a kind of symphony of tastes.

But this type of Italian-American cooking is different from that. Rather than bringing many ingredients together to form a new taste, or to have dishes with multiple and subtle layers of flavor, here, more often than not, we try to bring out the best taste of the thing in itself. In aglio e olio, it's the taste and aroma of olive oil and garlic, purely. In a beefsteak with olive oil and lemon, it's the rich taste of the meat. In linguine with shellfish, it's the briny taste of the oceans living in each clam or mussel. At its best, this kind of cooking lets you come to individual foods at their peak. I love the wonders of French cooking, with its multiplicity of sauces and flavors and preparations. But, here, things are simpler, perhaps more basic, but no less wonderful.

Pasta with Broccoli Rabe

Prepare broccoli rabe as directed in the chapter on vegetables. That is, wash, peel, and chop one large bunch of broccoli rabe and boil it until tender. When the rabe is just about done, in another saucepan heat a generous half-cup of olive oil with three or more large cloves of garlic, minced or mashed. Cook the garlic over low heat in the oil until it starts to take on color. Quickly, spoon the cooked rabe and a half-cup of its cooking water into the oil. Be careful of splatters. Simmer for a few minutes; add salt, pepper, and a large pinch of red pepper.

Bring a large pot of salted water to a rolling boil and add a pound of spaghetti, linguini, or tagliatelle. Have a large, heated bowl with a quarter-cup of olive oil ready to receive the pasta. When drained, add the pasta to the warm bowl and toss with the olive oil. Then add the oil and rabe sauce to the pasta.

Serve it in individual warm bowls with plenty of grated Parmesan, some coarse salt, and more red pepper for those who desire it.

White Clam Sauce

Spaghetti – or, more usually, linguini – with clams is one of the most singularly delicious dishes of any cuisine in any culture. To do it right is not particularly simple, but with a little care the results are superb. This recipe serves four people handily as a first course. Increase it proportionally to feed more.

Buy two dozen of the freshest small hardshell clams you can find. Such clams are usually marketed as littlenecks. Additionally, buy a half dozen or so cherrystone clams which, despite the seemingly petite character of their name, are actually much larger than littlenecks. You will be cooking these to add more clam juice to the sauce.

Your first task is to scrub the clams under running water until their shells are perfectly clean. A vegetable brush works fine. Discard any clams that are open and won't close when tapped against the countertop.

Now, in a heavy saucepan large enough to hold the clams easily, put a quarter-cup of olive oil and the clean clams. Cover tightly, and over medium-high heat shake the pan back and forth until the clams are all open. Try not to cook them for more than a minute after they open since they should be tender and just barely cooked, not chewy and rubbery.

If some obstinate clams refuse to open, take out the open ones with tongs, put them aside in a bowl, and shake the ones that remain closed over the heat until they relent. Discard any that refuse to open after this kind and gentle persuasion. The larger cherrystones may take a bit longer to open. Place all the open clams in a bowl leaving about a third of a cup or so of oil and broth in the pan. If it's much more, cook it down over medium heat until it is about a third of a cup.

Next, to remove any trace of sand, pour this broth into a bowl through the finest mesh strainer you have. If there's a fair amount of sand in the broth, check the open clams individually to see if one might be causing the problem. If so discard him, too.

Put a large pot of lightly salted water on for the linguini or spaghetti, either store-bought or home-made. Time everything so that the pasta and the incorporation of the oil and clam broth, which follows, finish at about the same time.

In a heavy two-or three-quart saucepan heat a generous half-cup of your finest olive oil with two or three cloves of garlic, crushed. As soon as the garlic is just lightly browned, add the strained clam broth. If you do this quickly it will help prevent splattering. Add some flakes of red pepper, a grinding or two of black pepper, but no salt. The clam broth should be salty enough. Since the object is to incorporate the oil and liquid as best we can, bring this oil, garlic, and broth mixture to a slow simmer and keep it there while the pasta cooks.

A minute or two before the pasta is ready, turn off the heat under the sauce and add the small littleneck clams, still in their shells, to the sauce. Gently stir them around to coat them all thoroughly. (What should you do with the larger cherrystones that you steamed with the others in order to have more broth? Well, you could chop their meat finely and add it to the sauce. Or you can do what I always do. Eat them there in the kitchen and throw away the shells so nobody knows what you did.)

When the pasta is just al dente, drain it in a colander and put it in a large bowl. Quickly, before the pasta starts to stick together, pour the sauce over it, holding back the clams. Mix gently, then pour the clams on the top. Sprinkle a healthy handful of chopped parsley over it all and serve at once.

At the table, each person takes a few clams in their shells along with a serving of pasta. Some people like to have a little Parmesan cheese to grate over their spaghetti. I think that the strong taste of cheese detracts from the sweet and delicate taste of the clam sauce. If it's your house, please discourage it.

Pasta and Squid

Before you begin, read the section on squid in the chapter on fish and shellfish (page 110). Then, in a half-cup of olive oil, lightly brown three crushed cloves of garlic. Add a few pinches of red pepper and about two pounds of cleaned squid, cut into rings, plus their tentacles. Lower the heat and cook slowly for about two minutes, until the squid is cooked but still tender. Remove the squid and cook the liquid down so that it's approximately three-quarters of a cup. As with clam sauce, the idea is to flavor the oil with the concentrated taste of the fish, not to make soup.

Cook a pound of linguini in six quarts of rapidly boiling water. When it's just al dente, drain it in a colander, put it in a large bowl, add the sauce and mix thoroughly. Spread the squid over the top. Olives and chopped parsley can be added as you bring it to the table.

Linguini Tutto Mare

This is what you serve to your best company. Putting it all together is not easy, and you should be totally comfortable with working with squid, clams, mussels, and shrimp before you attempt it. Since it involves so many ingredients, I've doubled the amount of pasta you'll use. This recipe easily feeds eight as a main course or 10 or more as a first.

First, clean about a pound of squid according to the directions in the section on squid. Cut the body into rings and the tentacles into bite-sized pieces and set aside.

Next, scrub two dozen small hardshell clams and scrub and debeard two dozen mussels. Set them all aside in separate bowls.

Then, take two dozen medium sized shrimp. You may peel and de-vein them or not, as you wish. Set them aside as well.

Finally, take either a pound of scallops, cleaned of any attached sand, or a pound of any boneless solid white fish such as sea trout, black bass, or striped bass. Cut the fish into pieces one inch square or less. Set this aside as well.

In a cup of olive oil fry three crushed cloves of garlic until very lightly golden brown. Add the clams, stir them around in the hot oil, cover and cook over medium-high heat until they all open. Remove them as soon as they're open, discarding any that stay closed. Set them aside and add the cleaned mussels to the oil and clam broth mixture in the pan. Cook them until they're open as well. This should all take about four minutes over medium-high heat. Remove them when done to their own bowl. Again, discard any that simply refuse to open.

Now lower the heat and bring the olive oil and shellfish broth to a simmer. Add the fish or scallops, the shrimp, and the squid. Cook this all at a bare simmer (Do not let this even come close to a boil!) until everything is just done. When ready, the shrimp should be pink and firm but not hard, and both the fish (or scallops) and the squid should be opaque. Remove everything with a slotted spoon and set aside in a bowl.

Now, over moderate heat, cook the oil and broth mixture down for about four or five minutes to concentrate the taste. It should cook down by about half.

In a large pot of boiling water cook two pounds of linguini al dente. As the pasta cooks, add all the ingredients back into the sauce and bring it close to a simmer. The point is not to cook the sauce further but to get it all hot to pour over the pasta.

When the pasta is ready, drain it well in a colander, put it in a very large bowl or on a platter, and pour the sauce over it, holding back the seafood. Put in enough sauce to coat the pasta thoroughly but not so much that it swims in the sauce. Mix the sauce and linguini thoroughly, then place the seafood over the top and sprinkle it all with a handful of chopped parsley. Serve at once.

Pesto

Tomato sauce was every-day, but pesto was special. It doesn't matter that today we tend to treat it like common mayonnaise, it still is special.

The following recipe goes lighter on the garlic than most, so the taste of the basil comes through more purely.

In a small, unoiled, heavy frying pan toast one-quarter cup of pine nuts (pignoli) over medium heat until they're very lightly browned. Better to use them under toasted or even untoasted than burnt in any way. Now put the pignoli into a blender or food processor with one medium clove of garlic, peeled and sliced. Blend until the pignoli and garlic are the consistency of cornmeal. Add to this one full cup of whole fresh basil leaves without stalk or stems. Blend until the leaves are thoroughly incorporated with the pignoli and garlic. Add a quarter teaspoon of salt and a grinding of black pepper, and, with the machine on, slowly add one-half cup of your best olive oil. Then add one-quarter to one-half cup of the finest, just-grated Parmesan cheese. Blend for a second and the pesto is done. You may, if you want, substitute fresh Italian parsley leaves for up to one-quarter cup of the basil.

Now, obviously, our grandparents didn't use a food processor when they went about making pesto. They ground the nuts and garlic and basil with a mortar and pestle — hence "pesto." That's still a good way to do it, though I'm not convinced it's appreciably better. If you want to try it, take the same ingredients as above and begin by grinding the toasted nuts, the garlic, and the salt and pepper in the mortar. When these ingredients are ground fine, mash in the basil leaves, chopped fine. Then slowly add the oil, grinding each tablespoon in to incorporate it. Stir in the grated cheese at the end.

Contrary to most other cookbooks, I don't think you should freeze pesto. The garlic and cheese become stronger as they sit, even when frozen. However, if you grow or inherit a great mass of basil at the end of the summer, you can grind up the basil and oil in the proportions given above, freeze it, and then add it to the proper amount of nuts, garlic, and cheese when you want to serve it later in the season.

I tell you this with some hesitation, even though over the years I've frozen my share of basil. Yes, there is something very sweet and satisfying about putting some pesto in a bowl of minestrone or even on some simple chicken broth in the midst of icy winter. But there's a special joy that comes with the first taste of summer basil, long awaited, long imagined, and maybe only dimly remembered. Like the first handful of raspberries in summer, it will never disappoint you. Even though commerce and science can now give us asparagus in the fall, strawberries in the winter, and oranges all the year through, there is something right about taking our foods as they grow in turn, and then living, for a while, on memory and expectation. The days are short enough anyway. So, yes, freeze some basil this year; but next year, don't. Tomato sauce you can eat every day; but pesto's worth waiting for.

Polenta

Cooking Polenta

Despite what fancy cookbooks tell you these days, when it comes to polenta nothing could be simpler.

In a large three- or four-quart saucepan, bring a quart and a half (six cups) of water and two teaspoons of salt to a boil. While stirring, slowly pour in one and one-half cups of either white or yellow cornmeal. (Depending on your taste, this can be either finely or more coarsely ground cornmeal. I tend to prefer the texture of the coarser grind over the smoothness of the more finely ground.) Reduce the heat so the polenta simmers and stir frequently with a strong wooden spoon so that it doesn't stick to the bottom and scorch. Although you will read that it's traditional to cook polenta for a minimum of 30 minutes, and sometimes as long as an hour, the truth is it's usually ready in less time than that. Still, cook it slowly for at least 15 minutes. Or follow the old trick of waiting till the polenta leaves the sides of the pot cleanly as it's stirred – then it's definitely done.

If you find that you have a heavy hand pouring the cornmeal into the boiling water and it makes lumps, then instead of bringing six cups of water to the boil bring only four to the boil and add the extra two cups of cold water directly into the cornmeal. Stir it about to make a slurry and then add that to the boiling water. Lumps? No lumps.

This is enough to serve six as a luncheon meal or as a first course, following one of the recipes below.

One note of caution: As it cooks, polenta bubbles and pops in the pot, throwing out hot bits of wet, scalding cornmeal. Wear long sleeves.

Polenta with Gorgonzola

This is one of the few recipes where Gorgonzola is used in a cooked dish. And few things could be simpler.

Merely ladle the hot polenta into individual heated bowls, stir into each a few tablespoons of crumbled Gorgonzola cheese, a sprinkling of salt, and a few grindings of black pepper. Drizzle some aromatic olive oil over the top and eat.

The same could be done with Parmesan. Simply stir a good handful of grated Parmesan into the piping hot polenta in place of the Gorgonzola. Straightforwardly enough, you now have "Polenta with Parmesan."

Or, if you want to be fancy (and smooth out the taste of the Gorgonzola or Parmesan at the same time) you can heat a half cup of mascarpone cheese, mix in the Gorgonzola or Parmesan over a very low flame, heat it through till it melts and melds, then add this cheese/mascarpone mix to the bowl with the polenta. (To be honest, I snuck both these in here because they are so marvelously delicious. Not a soul in the old neighborhood ever thought of making any such thing. Why not? See, below, the minor excursus on creamy and "white" (page 88).

Polenta and Tomato Sauce

In making this we simply substitute polenta for pasta. Spoon the soft polenta hot from the pot into individual bowls, cover with bubbling-hot tomato sauce, throw on a handful of grated Parmesan, and maybe some chopped parsley. Surround with the pieces of meat that cooked in the sauce.

Polenta with Sausages 1

As the polenta is simmering on the stove, fry up two or three fresh Italian sausages (mild or hot) per person. Spoon the hot polenta into individual bowls, surround it with the cooked sausages, and pour the sausage fat hot from the pan directly over the polenta. Add some olive oil if the sausages haven't given up enough fat. And if the polenta seems too bland, add some grated Parmesan. This is so delicious that it has to be very bad for you.

Polenta with Sausages 2

This is similar to plain polenta with sausages (above) except that some tomato sauce is added to the cooked sausage. As the polenta is cooking, fry up two or three fresh Italian sausages per person. Cut each sausage in two or three pieces before frying them. When they're done, add two cups of any previously made tomato sauce, pick up all the little brown bits clinging to the bottom of the pan with a flat wooden spatula, bring the sauce to the simmer and ladle it all over hot polenta in individual bowls. Serve it with grated Parmesan.

Fried Polenta

One reason for making more polenta than you can use all at once is so you can have fried polenta the next day.

Boil cornmeal for polenta as in the basic recipe. When done, pour it into either a large, flat pan like a jelly-roll pan or a bread pan. Rinse each with cold water just before adding the polenta, but do not dry — just shake off the excess water. Put in the polenta, spread it flat with a wet spatula, and refrigerate. It should be ready to fry in about two hours, longer for the more compact one in the bread pan. They will keep in the refrigerator for a few days. Cover them with a cloth or waxed paper.

To fry, cut the polenta in the flat pan into squares, or remove and slice the polenta in the bread pan into 1/4" slices, dust lightly with flour, and fry in hot oil or fat. Serve with tomato sauce, or use as a base for something like peppers and eggs, or have as a starch to accompany an unstuffed roast chicken.

Risotto

Here I go again being culinarily incorrect: I think risotto is one of the more over-rated dishes in Italian cooking. When it's not perfect, it's horrible (even its partisans agree with that); and (here I stand alone), even when it's perfect I don't think it's all that great. Give me a side of good old American rice, cooked fluffy, and covered with lightly browned butter, salt, and parsley any day. But, since everyone who cooks should, once a year, just for the practice, try to make a good risotto, here is the standard mode of preparation. If you disagree with me and love it, I'm happy for you.

First, make or defrost about a quart or a quart-and-a-half of homemade chicken stock and bring it to a slow boil. Grate two-thirds of a cup of Parmesan cheese and chop up about two handfuls of parsley leaves. Set them aside. Next, in a two-quart saucepan, heat two tablespoons of olive oil. In this, gently cook half a large onion, chopped, until just translucent. Add one-and-a-half cups of imported Italian rice (generally Arborio), coating it with the oil and onions in the pot. Now add a quarter-cup of the simmering stock, stirring slowly. When this is absorbed, add another quarter-cup, and continue to stir gently. The heat under the rice should be just enough to have the rice simmer in the stock ever so slowly while the stock is being absorbed by the rice. Keep repeating this for about 15 or 20 minutes until the rice is cooked, with just a hint of firmness in each grain. If it looks like you may run out of stock, you can finish the rice with some boiling water. Risotto should be creamy when done, leaning neither toward soupy on one end nor gummy on the other.

Immediately stir in the cheese, then the parsley, and serve. Depending on your stock, each person might need to add salt at the table.

More on Risotto: Peas, Asparagus, Porcini, Mushrooms, Shrimp …

Risotto comes with any number of variations, all pretty much based on the recipe above. For example, cooked peas or asparagus can be added to the oil-coated rice along with the first quarter-cup of hot stock. The peas (freshly shelled or frozen) should be pre-cooked in lightly salted water until tender, the asparagus peeled, cut into one-inch lengths, and either simmered in water or stock or fried in oil for about three minutes. If you simmer the asparagus in water or stock, use that liquid along with the chicken stock to make the risotto. Use the water from the peas as well. How many peas or how much asparagus to add depends on what you have available or how much you want to make.

Dried porcini mushrooms also make for a good variation on the basic recipe. For this, soak about a half-cup of dried porcini in two cups of very hot water. Let the mushrooms sit in this for at least a half-hour. Remove the softened mushrooms from the water and rinse them thoroughly under running water to work out any dirt and grit that might be lurking in the folds and pores. Dry them, chop roughly, and slowly sauté in a bit of olive oil for about five minutes. Add two cloves of finely minced garlic and sauté a few minutes longer, being careful not to burn the garlic. Add these to the oil-coated rice at the start of the basic recipe and add the liquid the porcini soaked in, strained, to the chicken stock. Proceed as above.

You can do the same with fresh, non-porcini mushrooms. Simply clean a dozen (or whatever reasonable number you wish) fresh mushrooms, slice and fry them with some garlic, add them to the rice at the start of the recipe, and continue as above. Obviously, here there will be no soaking liquid to add to the chicken stock.

Finally, you can add shrimp, fish, or squid to a risotto. For shrimp simply fry up a half pound or more of peeled and deveined shrimp, cut into one-inch lengths, in a little olive oil with some minced garlic. Contrary to the previous recipes, I'd add these to the rice at the end of the basic recipe, just before I add the last bit of stock. If you have a tomato or two on hand you could peel, core, squeeze and chop them in with the shrimp as they cook, putting both tomatoes and shrimp in with the rice toward the end.

For a fish risotto, choose about a pound of firm, white-fleshed, boneless fish, cut it into one-inch cubes, season it with salt and pepper and fry the pieces in olive oil over medium heat until they are just cooked through, perhaps about five or six minutes. (Some minced garlic added at the end so as not to burn it is a fine addition.) Add these pieces of fried fish to the risotto towards the end of the cooking of the rice, perhaps just before the last addition of stock. As with the shrimp, some tomato can be added to the fish as well. Note, also, that these various risotti with seafood still call for Parmesan cheese. This is one of the few places where you'll see cheese and seafood together. The rice seems to keep the taste of the cheese from overtaking the delicacy of the fish.

For risotto with squid, first read all about squid in the chapter on Fish and Shellfish (page 110). Then poach a pound of squid cut into ringlets and tentacles in barely simmering salted water for a few minutes, until just done and still tender. Add these to the risotto towards the end, again perhaps with the last addition or two of stock.

If you have it all — fish, shrimp, squid — add them all to the risotto. Note also that it's fine to make these risotti with fish or vegetable stock rather than chicken stock. If you want to make your own fish stock, be careful to use only fresh shrimp shells and/or the flesh and bones of white-fleshed and non-oily fish, simmering them in water with an onion, carrots, celery, parsley, salt, pepper and perhaps a few other herbs and mild spices for about an hour.

A Note on "White Foods"

Nope, this isn't a statement on Anglo cuisine; it's a discussion of the color "white." By now, the careful reader will have noticed that there's little in these recipes that's terribly "white" — no cream sauces, almost no melted cheeses, nothing. This is because my whole neighborhood thought eating something white would make you die. Well, at least everybody acted that way. The very thought of putting milk or cream in anything, even in something as Italian (though northern style) as Fettuccine Alfredo, verged on the suicidal. I still remember telling my mother, when I was away at college, that the cafeteria served a cream of mushroom soup and it was delicious. She said I should come right home because the people there were trying to kill me.

My guess is that this phobia has real roots in the lactose intolerance of so many southern Europeans. But, being Italian, everybody overcompensated. Coffee? Black only; no milk. Mayonnaise? Never! Cream cheese on a bagel? Only the slightest schemer, and then cover it up with something so you couldn't see it. Obviously, mozzarella and ricotta are white, but even there we'd fix it: You knew the pizza was done when the mozzarella on top had turned golden brown. Ricotta in the lasagna? Well, silly, that's why you cover each layer with tomato sauce, so it's no longer white. Even though turning milk to cheese destroys most of the troublesome enzymes, the worry was still there. But, in any event, "coloring" the white away made everyone feel a bit safer. Go figure.

Fish and Shellfish

Fish and Shellfish

Fish

We've become, these days, terribly fancy about fish. We buy halibut flown in from Alaska, salmon packed in ice and shipped overnight from Norway, and "orange roughy" manages to get to us somehow from somewhere in the South Pacific. And we pay an exorbitant price for every small bit. Who looks for bluefish anymore? Who buys mackerel or fluke or porgies? Well, we all should. They may not look as pretty sitting there on ice; they may seem common rather than fancy. Buy them anyway and have a feast.

Fried Fish Filets

It's almost an embarrassment to begin this chapter with so simple a dish, but, since it might be the best one of all, why not?

Buy the freshest filet of flounder or sole you can find. Yellowtail flounder, Dover, gray or lemon sole — all are just perfect. Use, generally, two filets per person, more if they're teenagers. Rinse each piece and pat dry.

Now, while you can put plain breadcrumbs on a plate, mix them with a bit of salt and pepper, and simply coat each filet with the crumbs, we would generally do this instead: On one plate put enough flour to coat lightly both sides of each filet. Next to it put a bowl in which you've beaten an egg with a teaspoon or so of water. Next to that put a plate with plain breadcrumbs seasoned with salt and pepper, as above. Finally, take each filet and dust it in the flour; then dip each lightly floured filet into the beaten egg, letting any excess egg drip off; then coat each filet in the crumbs. Set each coated filet aside for a few minutes to rest.

Why do all this? Because the flour will stick nicely to the damp fish, the egg will adhere to the flour, and the crumbs will meld nicely with the egged filets to make a good coating. Isn't the practical science behind cooking a marvel!

After the filets have rested for a few minutes, heat a quarter-cup of olive oil in a large skillet. When the pan is hot enough to sizzle the filets when added but not so hot as to burn them, add a few pieces of fish. When light brown, turn them over and brown them on the other side. Under no circumstances overcook the fish. Just remember that filets cook in moments.

Add more oil and more filets to the pan and continue till all are cooked. Have the rest of the meal completely ready when you start so that the fish can be served right from the pan.

Garnish with lemon wedges and chopped parsley.

Whole Baked Fish

Have the fish-monger scale and clean a two-pound firm-fleshed saltwater fish such as sea bass, striped bass, or bluefish. Leave on both the head and the tail.

When you're ready to cook, set your oven at 375°. Wash the fish under cold water and pat dry. Using your hands, rub olive oil over and in the fish, covering it well. Place the fish in an oiled baking dish or ovenproof platter.

In the cavity of the fish place a few different herbs or vegetables. For example, a sprig or two of fresh rosemary and some sliced lemons, or some thinly sliced onions mixed with a crushed clove or two of garlic, would do very well. Lightly salt the inside cavity. The seasonings you put in will not so much flavor the fish as perfume it slightly; the taste will still be of baked fish, with hints of oil and lemon.

Bake the fish for 10 minutes. As it cooks, mix a quarter-cup of olive oil with the juice of half a large lemon. After 10 minutes, turn the fish over and spoon half the oil and lemon mixture over it. In five more minutes, turn the fish again and pour the remaining oil and lemon over the fish. After five more minutes, remove the fish from the oven and test to see if it's done. If the flesh along the backbone separates easily with a knife and the flesh is opaque, the fish is done. If not, test again in another three to five minutes.

Serve the fish with lemon wedges and sprinkled with a handful of chopped Italian parsley.

A two-pound fish should satisfy four people.

Grilled Fish

You can grill a fish over a charcoal fire in a manner similar to cooking it in the oven. As above, have the market clean and scale a two-pound bass or bluefish. Or buy a few smaller fish, such as snapper, mackerel, or porgy. Mix a half-cup of olive oil with the juice of one lemon and a half teaspoon of salt. Marinate the fish in this for an hour or so, at room temperature, turning a few times.

Start the charcoal grill. When the coals are ready, move them to the side edges of the grill, since you will cook the fish, covered, over indirect heat. Having the coals directly under the fish is a sure-fire way to burn them rather than to cook them.

When the grill is ready, place the fish in the center, away from the hot coals. Cover and cook for 10 minutes. At the end of 10 minutes, test for doneness. Smaller fish should be ready by now; larger ones may take another three minutes or more.

As above, serve with lemon wedges and chopped parsley.

Pan-Fried Whole Fish

Since we now will be cooking in a frying pan, have the fish dealer behead the fish (unless they're very small) so that two or three of them will fit in the pan. Small fish like porgy are best for this recipe.

Unless they are very small, one fish will feed one person. Wash the fish under cool, running water and dry them thoroughly. Dust each with flour seasoned lightly with just salt and pepper. In a large frying pan or skillet, heat a quarter-inch of olive oil (or vegetable oil and a bit of butter) over medium-high heat. As soon as the oil smells fragrant, add the fish. Do not cover. If the fish are cooking too quickly, lower the heat and turn them often.

For fish that are about an inch thick at the meatiest, 10 minutes of cooking is just about right. Even though in Italy some restaurants consider it insulting to ask for lemon with your fish – as if you need it to cover over the taste of old fish – the truth is that a squeeze of lemon makes even the best fish taste better.

Two vegetables that seem to go exceptionally well with fried fish are spinach sautéed with garlic (page 191) and brazed fennel or finocchio (page 170).

Shrimp

Whether because they were too expensive or too much trouble, we had shrimp only rarely. The troublesome part is in shelling and de-veining them. Truthfully, however, it's no great breach of etiquette for anyone, even guests, to peel cooked shrimp at the table; and, unless they're jumbo sized, there's usually no need to de-vein shrimp at all.

If you want to remove the vein — it's actually not a vein at all but part of the shrimp's rather primitive digestive system — simply peel the shell off the shrimp, leaving it intact at the tail; then, with a sharp knife, make a shallow cut along the curved back to the tail. The vein, usually black, can then easily be lifted out. As I said, I generally don't peel shrimp before I cook them since I think the shell helps seal in moisture and flavor, but there's no real harm either way.

Since shrimp also seem to absorb water very easily, try to buy the freshest ones you can and don't wash them. Under no circumstances peel them under running water.

I'm tempted to say that you should avoid buying shrimp that has been "previously frozen." Depending on how they were frozen and, especially, how they were defrosted, their flavor can dissipate and their texture deteriorate. Once damaged, there is no way to cook flavor back into shrimp. But I do know that often frozen shrimp are the better or even only option. Still, if they're truly fresh — firm, sweet smelling, and soon off the boat — gravitate towards the "fresh shrimp."

Count on a half-pound of shrimp per person.

Boiled Shrimp

Bring about two quarts of lightly salted water to a boil. Add one sliced lemon, a few whole cloves, a bay leaf, six allspice, and six peppercorns. Simmer this for about 15 minutes, covered. Then add the shrimp, half a pound per person. Simmer this very gently for about five minutes or until the shrimp are just done. Under no circumstances whatsoever let them boil or they'll become tough and hard. I don't care that they're called "Boiled Shrimp," don't.

The shrimp are done when they're reddish on the outside and opaque white all the way through. Cooking time depends on how cold the shrimp were when you put them in the water, whether they're shelled or not, and their size. Look at them, check them, taste them. Slightly undercooked is fine. Overcooked cannot be fixed.

Drain the shrimp and put them in a good-sized bowl. Squeeze a lemon over them all, sprinkle with chopped parsley, and serve with extra lemon wedges. If unpeeled, everyone can peel their own at the table.

Shrimp with Oil and Lemon

This makes for a nice first course or a light lunch.

Poach one-quarter pound or more of unshelled shrimp per person either in barely simmering salted water or in water in which some aromatic spices have been added, as above. They should simmer until their shells have turned that pleasant shrimpy-red and their flesh is opaque. (Again, exactly how long this will take depends on how large the shrimp are, how cold they were when you put them in the liquid, and even how much water they're simmering in. If you have cookbooks that read like science manuals, with exact measurements and perfect timing, they're fakes. Don't read them.)

While the shrimp are poaching, mix one-half cup of rich olive oil, a small clove of garlic, crushed, a large pinch of salt, and the juice of one lemon. (This should be enough for up to about two pounds of shrimp.) Drain the shrimp and, while they are still hot, toss the shrimp with the oil and lemon mixture in a warm bowl. Let the shrimp sit in this, stirring occasionally, until they reach room temperature. As always, chopped parsley has a special affinity for oil, lemon, and garlic, so sprinkle some liberally over the top.

Fried Shrimp

We generally had these around the holidays, although they're simple enough to prepare anytime.

Completely shell and, if you wish, devein two pounds of very small, fresh shrimp. Dust them all very lightly in flour seasoned with a few shakes of pepper and salt. You can shake the shrimp in a colander to get rid of any excess flour.

In a large, heavy frying pan heat two tablespoons of olive oil. When the oil is very hot, add about one third of the floured shrimp. Shake and turn them so they cook quickly without burning. Depending on size, each batch should be cooked in about one minute. When they're done, remove them to a bowl lined with paper towel. Heat more oil and fry the remaining batches the same way. Serve them at once, piping hot, with lemon wedges.

Grilled Shrimp

Done in the broiler or, especially, on the outdoor charcoal grill, this is probably the best way to prepare shrimp that there is.

A few hours before you're ready to grill, mix in a bowl two pounds of large, unshelled shrimp with a generous one-quarter cup of olive oil; four sprigs of fresh rosemary leaves stripped from their stems and roughly chopped (or two teaspoons dried, lightly crushed); three cloves of garlic, crushed; a half-teaspoon of salt; a good amount of freshly ground black pepper — at least a full teaspoon — and the juice of one lemon. The shrimp can sit in this for two hours at room temperature or they can be refrigerated overnight. Stir them up occasionally to keep them all well coated.

If the shrimp have been refrigerated, allow them to return to room temperature before you cook them. If you're broiling them, put the shrimp and their marinade in a low baking dish all in one level. Turn the broiler on high and cook them close to the flame with the broiler door ajar. When they're done on one side, turn them with a pair of tongs or long-handled fork.

On the charcoal grill, put the shrimp directly on the grate, turning them over and over with a long-handled turner until they're done. Depending on size, the whole process should take less than five minutes. If you're cooking them on the charcoal grill, either buy the largest size you can to keep them from slipping through the grate or hold six or eight together with bamboo skewers. Double skewering them makes turning even easier. Sprinkle with chopped parsley and serve with lemon wedges. With some rice and a salad, this makes a superb light meal.

Shrimp Scampi

"Shrimp scampi" is tied with "pizza pie" for this country's Italian Culinary Tautology Award.

In any event, "scampi" is not much different than the previous recipe except that it's done in a frying pan rather than over a grill.

In a large pan over medium heat, lightly brown two cloves of crushed garlic with a sprig of fresh rosemary (or half a teaspoon lightly crushed dried rosemary) in one-quarter cup of olive oil. Add the shrimp, either peeled or not, along with a quarter teaspoon of salt, a half teaspoon of crushed oregano, and a half teaspoon or more of freshly ground black pepper. Stir them constantly as they cook. When just done, add the juice of one lemon, let it simmer for a few seconds, and remove from the heat. Toss in a handful of chopped parsley. Serve in a large bowl with crusty Italian bread.

Even though everyone has to peel his own at the table, this makes a truly fine first course.

Baked Stuffed Shrimp

This is a quintessential New England Italian-American dish. It comes as close to baked stuffed lobster as you can get without a lobster.

Look for very large, impeccably fresh shrimp — ones that weigh about eight to a pound are fine. If these are unavailable, buy the largest shrimp you can afford. With a very sharp small knife cut the shell along the back of the shrimp, from where the head once was down to the tail. If you look inside the slit you have just made you can now fairly easily remove the vein. Do not— repeat, do not — remove the shell or the tail.

You now have a shrimp with its shell split along its back from shoulder (if shrimp have shoulders) to tail. With the "leggy" part of each shrimp resting on a cutting board, take your small sharp knife and gently cut down into the meat of the shrimp where you made the slit, from top to tail. Your aim is not to cut the shrimp in half but to keep it connected at the bottom while "butterflying" it out at the top. When done, each shrimp should be splayed open like a book, still connected at the bottom and still encased in its shell. Place the shrimp side-by-side in an ovenproof baking dish just large enough to hold them with scrunching too much.

Pre-heat your oven to medium-hot, about 375°.

The next step is to make the stuffing which will sit on top of the raw, newly splayed shrimp.

Crumbs from fresh or, especially, day-old bread are the best for the stuffing, though crumbs from stale bread are still acceptable. You can certainly use the coarser side of a grater to make crumbs, but the food processor makes everything much easier. Simply put a few handfuls of broken-up pieces of fresh, day-old, or stale bread into the bowl of the processor and run until the bread is cut to about the size of your pinky fingernail. (Bread that's fully stale will want to break up into finer crumbs. This is ok.) If you use store-bought crumbs (why?), make sure they are labeled "unseasoned," since we'll be doing the "seasoning" ourselves.

How much stuffing should you make? Well, that depends on the number and size of the shrimp you have. Let's assume that eight very large shrimp will feed four people as a main course. For that amount you'll need about two cups of coarse crumbs, or probably only a cup of fine crumbs. Season these crumbs with about a half teaspoon of salt, a half teaspoon freshly ground black pepper, and two crushed cloves of fresh garlic. In my opinion, the best herb to add, if you have it, is tarragon. Fresh is slightly superior to dried, but either will do. Add about two heaping tablespoons of chopped fresh tarragon or one scant tablespoon of dried. If you don't have tarragon, two tablespoons of chopped fresh basil will also do fine. Add a small handful of chopped Italian parsley too.

To this dry mixture of crumbs/salt/pepper/garlic/tarragon or basil/parsley now add up to one stick of melted butter. (New England Italians use butter with greater abandon than we New Yorkers. We'd tend to moisten the crumbs with oil. You can, too.) The point is to dampen the crumbs without making them sodden. Lightly mix the crumbs as you add the melted butter and stop if it seems to be getting too wet. The aim is to have something that's light yet moist enough to retain its shape when spooned onto the shrimp.

Now taste the stuffing. Does it need more salt? Pepper? Garlic? The amounts given above are moderate just so you can use your own judgment and bring it to suit your taste.

With a tablespoon and your fingers, put a large mound of stuffing on top of each shrimp. Don't skimp; pile it up. You want the stuffing to be light and crumbly while still retaining its shape.

If there's any leftover melted butter, pour it around the sides of the shrimp. Or add a half-stick of butter, cut in pieces, around the shrimp. Or you can add a little olive oil, say, a quarter cup. This not only helps the shrimp cook, but it will also give you a bit of sauce to spoon over any rice or noodles you might make to go with the dinner.

Put the stuffed shrimp in the pre-heated oven. How long they take to cook depends on their size, how cold they were when they went in, and how thick the stuffing is. I'd check after six minutes or so, though they will more likely take about 10 minutes. What you want to see is that the shrimp have just lost their grey-translucent color and have become opaque-white. To do this checking you will probably, carefully, have to peek a bit under the stuffing. When done you may want to put them under the broiler for a second to brown the top of the crumbs.

This makes for a memorable dinner when served with rice, a green salad, and candles. Garnish the plate with lemon to drizzle over the shrimp, and spoon any sauce in the bottom of the baking dish over the rice.

Squid

I know that hardly anyone buys whole, uncleaned squid these days. Indeed, finding whole squid anywhere is probably only slightly easier than finding gold. But if you live near the coast and you do find some — and you'd like to try your hand at cooking "from scratch," as is said — here's how to begin:

First, when you buy whole squid at the fish market it should look firm, not flabby, with clean eyes and the smell of only the sea.

Second, know that cleaning squid separates the men from the boys: men usually hate it; boys find it interesting. For those of you unashamed of the bravado of youth, read on ....

Take the cylindrical body of the squid in one hand and, holding the head and tentacles with the other, pull. Out should come all the internal parts of the squid attached to the tentacles. Set all this aside for now.

The squid body in your other hand is shaped like a torpedo with fins. Inside is something that looks like a quill pen made of cellophane. This "quill" — that's actually what it's called, too — is the equivalent of the squid's backbone. Pull it out, wash it off and show it to the kids, who'll be fascinated the first time, but never again. Under cool running water take off as much of the mottled reddish skin that covers the body as will come off easily. Squid has a reputation for toughness and leaving the skin on tends to keep the meat rubbery. Remove as much of it as you can without being fanatical. Remove also the "wings" on the side of the body and put them aside for later.

Now, turn the squid body inside out. Often the best way is to push with your index finger from the pointed end up through the middle. You have to reverse the body cylinder in order to wash out the inside cavity. Wash away any sand and any internal parts that didn't come out with the tentacles. Remove any loose membrane.

Lay the tentacles on the cutting board and cut them off just in front of the creature's somewhat plaintive eyes.

Save the tentacles; discard the rest. This means getting rid of everything from the eyes back to all the internal organs. Out. All of it.

Now, take the tentacles and look at the place where you made the cut. Depending on where you cut, there may be a sharp, bony beak – like a small parrot's beak – buried among the tentacles. (Despite their air of innocence and helplessness on the fish-monger's bed of ice, squid are really nasty little neighbors in the sea community.) After showing this to the kids, too, discard the beak altogether. You now have what looks like a grass skirt made of tentacles – a waistband with legs hanging down. Pick off as much skin as you easily can, again without being overly fastidious. The squid is now ready for use.

Fried Squid or Calamari Fritti

The easiest way to fry up some squid is simply to slice the cylindrical body into rings, dry all the pieces, including the tentacles, on a cloth or paper towel, shake them in some salted flour, and drop the pieces in a quarter-inch of olive oil over moderate heat. When they've turned golden, drain on paper towels, salt and eat. The only tricks are to wear an apron, because the squid will always pop and spit oil, and not to crowd the pan whatsoever. Once fried, you can squeeze some lemon over them, too.

If you'd like a variation on this, try flouring the squid pieces, shaking off the excess, dipping the pieces in an egg whipped up to a froth with a tablespoon or two of water, and shaking the newly egged pieces in some very fine dry breadcrumbs. Fry them up just as above.

Squid Salad

This is the calamari equivalent of the recipe for shrimp with oil and lemon given before.

Clean two to three pounds of fresh squid or buy it already cleaned at the market. If it's been cleaned at the market, it's still a good idea to inspect the squid for sand and (if the body of the squid is still whole) turn the bodies inside out to wash away any remaining internal parts. Split the "skirt" of tentacles in half, lengthwise, and cut the body into one-half-inch rings.

Before you cook the squid, make the dressing. In a bowl combine a generous one-third cup of olive oil, a mashed clove of garlic, the juice of one lemon, a handful of chopped parsley, a half teaspoon of salt and a liberal grinding of black pepper. Set the bowl aside until the squid is cooked.

Bring at least four quarts of salted water to the simmer. Put all the squid into the water and simmer it ever so slowly until it is completely opaque. This should take around five minutes. Please be careful — if the water comes to a boil, the squid flesh will clutch and become hard and rubbery. You want to keep the water barely at the simmer so as to gently poach, not boil, the squid.

Drain the squid and, while it's still hot, add the lemon-oil-parsley dressing. Stir it up frequently and let it come to room temperature before serving. It makes for either a fine first course or a light lunch. If there's dressing in the bottom of your dish, dip it up with some bread.

Baked Stuffed Squid

Although this could easily be served by itself as a light meal, it's usually prepared with pasta and served as the main part of a dinner. With a pound of pasta, this recipe will feed four.

Clean thoroughly four large squid. Coarsely chop the tentacles and the "wings" that you removed from the sides of the squid. Let all this sit on paper towels while you prepare the rest of the recipe.

In a large frying pan over low heat cook two onions coarsely chopped, and two crushed cloves of garlic in two tablespoons of olive oil. When the onion has become soft and translucent, add the chopped tentacles and "wings." Cook two minutes, stirring.

To this oil-garlic-onion-squid mixture add two cups of fresh breadcrumbs, a handful of chopped parsley, about two tablespoons of fresh basil, tarragon or a teaspoon of oregano, a quarter-teaspoon salt, and a half teaspoon of freshly ground pepper. Mix this over medium heat for about one minute, then set it aside.

After the stuffing has cooled a bit, add to it one thoroughly beaten egg and two tablespoons of grated Parmesan cheese. Now, with your fingers, gently fill the squid bodies with this stuffing. Fill the cylinders completely but without packing them too tightly or they'll burst as they cook. When they are all filled, either sew up the opening or thread it closed with a toothpick or piece of a bamboo skewer.

In a large frying pan with a close-fitting cover, heat two tablespoons olive oil over medium heat. Add the stuffed squid and fry them lightly on all sides until they're just lightly browned. Add a large can of crushed or pureed tomatoes. Bring this to a simmer on top of the stove, scraping up any brown bits clinging to the bottom of the pan. Then cover it and place it in a three-hundred-degree oven to simmer slowly for one hour.

To serve, remove the threads or toothpicks and cut the squid into slices about one-quarter inch thick. Pour the tomato sauce over one pound of macaroni, and serve the sliced, stuffed squid on the side.

This recipe can easily be cooked a day or two ahead. Simply save the squid in the refrigerator, covered in their sauce. Before slicing and serving, heat it slowly in a warm (250°) oven for an hour and pour over the just-cooked macaroni.

Baccala

Baccala is nothing more than dried, salted cod. It comes in little wooden boxes usually from Canada. You'll also see in Italian markets dried fish hanging by their tails from the rafters. This, too, is cod, but dried, not salted. Its more official name is "stockfish" ("stoccafisso," to be Italian about it.) (Italians are always doing this to good non-Italian words. For years I thought the Italian word for a bathroom was "baccousa." Only later did I realize that it was just a transformation of "back-house." Ya'gotta love a language like that.)

Back to the fish. Both baccala and stockfish are used in much the same recipes, though stockfish — the unsalted, air-dried cod — is much harder and drier than baccala proper, and it cooks up chewier.

To prepare both fish, they must be soaked for extended periods of time. Put the salted baccala in a large bowl of cool water and refrigerate it for up to two days, changing the water about three times a day. Stockfish is considerably more problematic. First, you must saw it into pieces. Yes, saw it. It cannot be either cut or broken. Saw it into four or five pieces. Soak it, refrigerated, in a large bowl or pot for at least five days, changing the water at least three times a day. And, no, it's not gone bad; it always smells fishy like that.

Both baccala and stockfish then need to be simmered in water — 15 minutes for the baccala; at least 30 minutes or more for the stockfish. For both, I usually put two or three large cloves of peeled garlic in with the water. Since stockfish has never been salted, you should salt its simmering water. The baccala water probably won't need any salt.

This simmering all needs to be done before proceeding further with any recipe.

Baccala Mantecato

Like many former poverty foods – polenta, broccoli rabe, pasta and beans – this has been taken over by new, upscale restaurants, given a French name ("brandade"), and sold in small portions for high prices. But it's still nothing more than reconstituted salt cod with olive oil. It's also absolutely delicious.

After soaking one box of the cod for a day or two, cut it into four-inch chunks and simmer it for 15 minutes or so (as above). Remove the pieces, saving some of the water. Put the pieces in a fairly large metal bowl, pick out any bones, and let them cool for a minute or two. In the meanwhile, finely chop one or two cloves of garlic and a small handful of parsley. If you simmered a few cloves of garlic with the fish, you can use them instead of the raw cloves for a milder garlic taste. Now, put the chopped parsley and garlic in the bowl with the fish and beat the mixture with a wooden spoon until it starts to get pasty. (You can use a hand mixer on slow or medium speed if you don't want to work for your dinner. To be honest, it's almost as good.)

When the fish starts to stick together, drizzle about a half-cup of very good olive oil, beating it as you go. You can also add a few tablespoons of the water the fish simmered in, if you managed to save any of it. (This tends to make the dish creamier, so go by whether you want that or not.) Now, taste it. If it needs salt, add it sparingly. Pepper, too, if you wish. The result should be a fairly grainy paste. That's it! Serve it surrounded with parsley leaves as a first course, with some good bread. Or it makes a fine light lunch with fried polenta on the side.

You can do much the same with stockfish. The final result is somewhat grainier, although it might have more character. After simmering about a pound of the reconstituted stockfish for half an hour, remove the fish from the water, reserve some of the water, and throw out any stray bones and skin. Put the pieces in a food processor with two cloves chopped garlic (or garlic that you simmered with the fish), a handful of coarsely chopped parsley, and three or four anchovy fillets or a scant teaspoon of coarse salt. Chop the fish in the food processor briefly, until it just about starts to hold together, then drizzle in between a half-cup to a cup of very good olive oil, mixing as you go. Taste the mixture for salt, add pepper if you'd like, and add some of the reserved cooking water if you want to bind the mixture together more. (Yes, using a food processor is quite new-fangled, but unlike with baccala it works fine here with the stockfish.)

You want to avoid making paste out of the fish, but true stoccafisso usually has enough body that this won't happen unless you terribly over-mix. As with baccala, serve on a plate as a first course with bread, surrounded by parsley and maybe a few lemon wedges or with fried polenta as a lunch.

Stockfish Salad

If you buy a whole stockfish, you will have a lot for a long time. (Since it keeps forever dried, you might want to think about only reconstituting it a piece at a time. By "piece" I mean one of the four or five pieces you sawed it into when you bought it.) Stockfish salad is simply that piece of stockfish reconstituted, then simmered for half an hour to an hour, flaked while still warm into a bowl with a half-cup of olive oil and the juice of a lemon, tossed, salted and peppered to taste and served as an antipasto. Remember that stockfish retains its chewy texture even after you've soaked it for a week and simmered it for an hour. It's just that way.

Baccala Fish Stew

Take about a pound of your reconstituted and simmered stockfish or a pound of your soaked and simmered salt cod, flaked or cut into bite-size pieces and set aside. In a fairly large saucepan, in about a quarter-cup of good olive oil, sauté a chopped carrot, a chopped celery stalk, a chopped onion, and two finely chopped cloves of garlic. Cook this until the vegetables are wilted or even slightly brown. Add two or three peeled, seeded, and chopped tomatoes, and cook it down for a few minutes. Now add a tablespoon of flour and cook it all, stirring, for another minute or two.

Now add the fish, about a quart and a half of water, a few sprigs of parsley tied with a string, and some salt. You can certainly use some of the water you simmered the baccala in, provided it's not too salty. Simmer it all very slowly for at least half an hour. While this is simmering, peel and dice three or four medium boiling potatoes. Add to the simmering stew and cook until the potatoes are tender. Remove the parsley. Taste for salt.

Serve this in individual bowls over a piece of stale or toasted Italian bread, or with toasted bread on the side. Sprinkle with chopped parsley.

This should serve six as a first course or four as a dinner.

Clams

Baked Stuffed Clams

Buy three dozen large hardshell clams, usually referred to as cherrystones. (One would think that something called "cherrystones" would be small. But, as we said before, at about three inches wide, they're not particularly tiny. "Littlenecks" is the name of hard clams smaller than cherrystones – and "chowders" are larger, often up to six inches or more across.)

If you're adept at opening clams, wash and open all you bought, saving the juice in a bowl for other uses. Drain and chop the clam meat fairly finely. If you're not so good at shucking, wash the clams thoroughly, put them in a large roasting pan with a half-cup or so of water and roast, covered if possible, in a hot (400°) oven until they all open. Discard any that refuse to open, though if they were all closed tight when you washed them, they all should be fine. You might want to try opening the recalcitrants with a shucking knife. Drain the clams, save the juices, and chop the clam meat to about the size of your pinkie fingernail.

Put a dozen slices of bacon on to fry slowly as you proceed. You'll want to turn the bacon off just as it is slightly cooked. You do not want the bacon crisp.

In a large frying pan, cook three or four minced garlic cloves and one onion, finely chopped, in a third of a cup of olive oil. As the garlic starts to color and the onion turns translucent, add a third of a cup of dry unflavored breadcrumbs and a handful of either chopped Italian parsley or a handful of chopped basil leaves, or, preferably, both. To this add the chopped clam meat. Season lightly with salt and more heavily with black pepper. Some red pepper flakes can be added as well if you want the clams to be somewhat spicy.

Remove the stuffing from the heat as soon as you've added the clams. Depending on how firm or loose you'd like the stuffing to be, you could add a beaten egg yolk or two once the stuffing is taken from the heat, placed in a large mixing bowl, and cooled slightly.

Take half the clam shells, clean off any pieces of clam muscle, mound a spoonful of the clam-stuffing mixture on each half-shell, drape a small piece of bacon over each stuffed clam (about a third of a slice on each), put the clams in a shallow roasting pan or two, and bake in a hot (400°) oven for 10 minutes or until the stuffing looks lightly brown and the bacon is cooked. Serve with lemon wedges as part of an antipasto or as the first course in a gala seafood dinner.

Clam Broth

Since you saved the juice that came from the clams you might as well use it. Bring the saved juice to a simmer and skim off any froth. Add an equal portion of water and bring it again to the simmer. If you put some of this in a Styrofoam cup and drop in a poached clam, you'll think you're standing in Coney Island, at Nathan's.

Meat, Chicken, and Eggs

Meat, Chicken, and Eggs

My grandparents ate very little meat. Whether this came from poverty or choice, I don't know. Probably it was both. In any event, meat was often more a flavoring in something — like meatballs in tomato sauce or spareribs in greens — than a dish in itself. If they each ate more than a pound of meat a week, I'd be surprised.

My mother, being more American, cooked meat more often; in fact, almost every day other than Fridays. Here's what comes from both generations.

Beef

Except maybe for meatballs, which we had at least once a week, we ate less beef in our house than we did chicken or pork. Sure, a beef braciola is good; but is it better than a beautiful roast pork or a sausage sandwich with peppers and onions, or a fragrant lemon-scented chicken? Hard questions. Though crusty meatballs hot from the fry pan, or a rare porterhouse with lemon and rosemary might tip the scales occasionally to beef.

Meatballs

Refer to the recipe for meatballs with sauce on page 41. I mention it here only to remind us that meatballs, cooked in sauce or just plain fried, make wonderful sandwiches. Remove much of the soft white part from a long piece of Italian bread (to make room for the meatballs), make a sandwich, and take it to work in a paper bag. As the aroma permeates the room, smile when your co-workers offer to trade you their yogurt.

Steak Pizzaiola

This is steak cooked like chicken cacciatore, although the resulting tomato sauce will be somewhat stronger and more delicious.

Since it combines two wonderful things – sufficient marbling and low price – I'm convinced that the best cut of steak for this dish is chuck. A chuck steak weighing about two pounds, about an inch-and-a-half thick, should feed four people easily.

Preheat your oven to 325°. In a heavy frying pan heat one-quarter inch of oil over medium-high heat. Dry the steak thoroughly with paper towels so that it will brown up nicely and not steam in the frying pan. When the oil is hot enough to sizzle the steak, add it, turning it frequently so that the outside cooks to an even chocolate brown. All you need to do is sear the outside of the steak till it's brown and crusty – the inside will cook in the sauce. Put the steak, still rare or medium rare, aside, collecting any juices that accumulate.

Pour off the oil that remains in the pan and pick up the brown bits stuck to the bottom by adding a half-cup of either beef or chicken stock. As this simmers, add a can of chopped or crushed tomatoes, some salt, pepper, the accumulated steak juices, and, if you'd like, a teaspoon of dried oregano. You can crush in a clove or two of garlic as well. Put the steak in a baking pan just large enough to hold it and the sauce, cover, and bake it for at least an hour, or until the steak is tender when pierced with a fork. If it seems that the sauce is getting too thick or drying out too much, add more stock.

Remove the steak from the pan, slice it against the grain, and serve it with a green salad or broccoli rabe plus a side of pasta, with the sauce spooned over the pasta.

Steak with Olive Oil and Lemon

This is more a northern Italian specialty than a Neapolitan dish, but it's simple and simply delicious.

Heat a heavy iron skillet on high until almost smoking, film it lightly with oil and immediately put in the nicest porterhouse, sirloin, or rib eye steak you can buy.

As with all meats that we wish to brown, dry the steak thoroughly and completely with paper towels since any moisture on the surface will cause it to steam a bit and prevent it from browning nicely. Sear the steak over high heat until crusty brown; then turn it over and sear the other side. Remove the steak and drizzle it with your best olive oil, squeeze some lemon over it, and sprinkle chopped rosemary on top. Salt and pepper to taste. If the steaks are small, do one per person; otherwise cook fewer, cutting them into appropriate portions when serving.

This is a steak traditionally served rare. If you must, cook it to medium-rare — but no further.

For a more American touch, you can always cook these steaks outside, over a very hot charcoal grill, instead of over the kitchen stove.

Chicken

Roast Chicken with Lemon

A plump chicken, scented by lemons, with a sauce flavored with lemon and rosemary, may well be the best Sunday dinner there is.

Preheat your oven to 350°. Wash and dry a good-sized chicken, between three and four pounds. Next, take two lemons and roll them a few times on the countertop to soften them and help them release their fragrance. Puncture each lemon with a fork about 10 times and place both lemons in the cavity of the chicken. If you have a sprig or two of fresh rosemary, put this in with the lemons as well. Tie the chicken's legs together with some string so that the poor bird won't come out of the oven looking like a failed ballerina. Rub the chicken liberally with oil or softened butter, put it on a rack in a baking dish, and roast for 40 minutes.

(A trick: If you think you can do it without mangling the front end of the bird, neatly try to cut out the wishbone before you cook the chicken. If you get it all out, slicing the breast into even, full slices is much, much easier.)

As it cooks, use a bulb baster to baste the chicken with any oil or melted butter that collects in the pan. You may wish to squeeze a lemon into the pan oils and baste the chicken with that. After 40 minutes, raise the heat in the oven to 400° and let the chicken cook and brown for another 15 minutes. When the drumsticks move easily in their sockets and the juice that flows from the thigh area when poked with a fork runs clear (not pink), the bird is ready.

Remove the cooked bird from the oven, untie its legs, and discard the lemons and rosemary in the cavity. (Make sure the juices that flow from the cavity are not still pink. If they are, the bird needs a few more minutes in the oven.) Set the chicken aside for a minute while you make the sauce.

With the roasting pan over a low flame on top of the stove, squeeze and strain the juice of one lemon into the oil and browned bits clinging to the bottom of the pan. Add any juice that drips from the waiting chicken and a quarter-cup rich chicken stock as well. Bring this all to the simmer, scraping up all the flavorful brown bits. Pour this into a gravy boat, skim off any fat that seems excessive, and serve this sauce with slices of the chicken.

Plain white American rice, with some of the lemon-flavored chicken sauce drizzled over it, and a spinach or arugula salad, are all that's needed to make this a feast.

Baked Chicken with Lemon

This is a simpler, though less perfect, recipe for lemoned chicken than the one above.

Have the butcher halve or cut up a three pound chicken, or purchase whatever parts you and your family prefer. Wash and dry each piece thoroughly. Film the bottom of a baking dish with oil or butter and sprinkle on some chopped rosemary leaves, fresh or dry. With your hands, generously oil or butter each chicken piece, lay them in the pan, and add a bit more rosemary and some salt. Thinly slice a lemon and place the pieces here and there over the chicken.

Put the chicken in a preheated 350° oven and bake it for about 40 or 45 minutes, or until the meatiest piece or joint is no longer pink. Every 10 minutes or so while it bakes, baste the pieces with whatever juices collect in the pan, with some melted butter, or with the juice of a fresh lemon.

When the chicken is done, set it aside and make some lemon-flavored sauce following the instructions for roast chicken, above.

You could use tarragon, fresh or dry, rather than rosemary, if you prefer.

Chicken Cacciatore

Chicken cacciatore is just chicken pieces cooked in the oven in a tomato sauce. Besides tasty chicken, you also wind up with a flavorful sauce that you can put on any spaghetti you might have as a side.

Buy however many pieces of chicken you'll need to feed your family that night. Count on about two pieces per person, excluding small parts like wings.

You can oil the chicken parts and put them in a baking dish, as in the recipe for baked chicken with lemon, above; but I prefer to fry them first, to crisp them up just a bit. To do so, wash, dry, and lightly flour each piece. In a large frying pan heat a one-quarter inch of oil over medium-high heat. When the oil is hot enough for the chicken to sizzle, put a few pieces in the pan and fry them until each piece is lightly brown on each side. You are not cooking the chicken here, only browning it. As they brown, put the pieces in a bowl or on a plate. Don't use paper towels since you'll want to add any juices that collect in the bowl into the tomato sauce.

When all the pieces are browned, place them flat in a baking pan. Pour off most of the fat from the pan and pick up the brown bits on the bottom by adding a half-cup of chicken stock over medium heat, scraping it all together with a spatula or flat wooden spoon. To this add one can of crushed canned tomatoes, some salt, and any juices that might have collected from the chicken pieces as they sat. Bring this to a simmer, pour over the chicken, and bake it all in a preheated 350° oven for 35 or 40 minutes. Test the largest piece for doneness.

Remove each chicken piece from the sauce, make some thin spaghetti as a side dish, spoon on some sauce from the chicken, snip on some fresh basil if you have it, and serve. Notice that if you want the taste of the chicken to come through in the sauce, avoid adding all the usual ingredients — no garlic, no tomato paste, no onions, no Parmesan on top. Just chicken flavored sauce, perhaps scented with some snips of fresh basil.

Pork

Roast Pork

A rib roast or loin roast of pork, flavored with garlic and rosemary, makes another great Sunday dinner. Again, there's nothing very complicated about its preparation.

Preheat the oven to 350°. Cut three or four cloves of garlic into thin slivers and strip a handful of rosemary leaves from their stems. On the top of a four- or five-pound roast, make a number of puncture holes with a sharp knife.

These holes should be deep enough to allow you to insert a sliver of garlic and a few rosemary leaves almost completely in. Do exactly that. Grate some black pepper and sprinkle some coarse salt over the top and set it in a baking dish in the middle rack of a pre-heated oven.

Now comes the $64 question: "How long do I cook it?" Well, from this distance, it's hard to say. Is the roast right from the fridge or has it come to room temperature? A cold roast will take much longer to cook, and the outside will dry out before the center is cooked. Also, how often do you open the oven door to check up on it? How well does your oven keep heat? Besides, how well calibrated is your oven? An oven that says 350° might actually be 20 degrees higher or lower.

So, how long do you cook it? Until the juices run slightly pink to clear, when the roast is pricked deeply with a fork. More exactly, cook it until an instant-read meat thermometer measures 140° to 145° when set into the very center of the roast. If you then remove the roast from the oven and let it sit for 10 or 15 minutes to compose itself before being sliced, the temperature should rise another five to ten degrees. (If you don't let it rest, it will stop cooking as soon as you slice into it and, most seriously, the delicious juices of the roast will come out rather than infuse themselves back into the meat.) This also gives you some time to finish up the rest of the meal.

Now, I must confess that this is not how pork was cooked back in the '50's. Back then, trichinosis was a threat, a threat that everyone needed to take seriously. There was a major sign up in our meat market that said in red block letters, in Italian, that "All meat of the pig has to be completely and thoroughly cooked." This meant completely.

The USDA recommended cooking it to 160°, which, of course, meant that by the time you sliced into it the meat was probably over 170° and fit only for use as building material.

But we now recognize a) that because of modern husbandry, trichinosis is no longer found in American pigs; b) that when pork is frozen, as almost all American pork is before you buy it, the freezing kills trichinosis; and most importantly c) that temperatures above 135° kill all traces of trichinosis. So, if you cook pork to 140° or 145°, and then let it rise to 150° or more, you're safe.

If you're still uneasy with this, cook it to 150°, then let it sit. But remember, pork that's still a little pink is eaten every day by thousands of Americans, and they all live to tell their co-workers what a great dinner they had the night before!

While the roast is cooking, you can either baste it periodically with the fat that accumulates in the pan or you can use that fat to oven roast some potatoes along with the pork. To do this, peel about one or two potatoes per person and cut them into quarter-inch slices or wedges. Oil them or drip some melted fat or lard over them (since the pork will most likely not have given up any fat yet), and place them in the oven dish around the pork. Turn and baste them regularly.

Depending on how long it takes the meat to cook, the potatoes might or might not be cooked when the roast is ready to come out. If they're not, remove the roast from the pan, raise the oven heat to 375° and continue to cook the potatoes until they are browned and tender. Salt and pepper them, sprinkle some rosemary in with them, and serve them on the side of the roast. Any kind of cooked greens – broccoli, broccoli rabe, chard, spinach – would be perfect with this.

Sausage

Here's where I prove again that this "Mediterranean Diet" cookbook is not a diet book as that term is usually used.

First, sausage meat. Buy about two pounds of pork – country ribs, Boston butt, pork stew meat – to be honest, inexpensive and fatty is much better than costly and lean. Ask the butcher for an additional pound of hard pork fat as well. Sorry to say, pork sausage that's too lean tastes a little like flavored sawdust.

To be clear as to the ingredients and measurements, let me offer the following list –

  2 pounds pork
  1 pound pork fat
  2 teaspoons of coarse salt
  1 tablespoon of ground black pepper
  2 tablespoons of crushed coriander seed
  2 tablespoons (scant) fennel seed OR 1 tablespoon red pepper and 2 -3 crushed cloves of garlic
  1 – 2 handfuls of chopped Italian parsley (optional)

The old-fashioned and perhaps best way to make sausage meat is to chop the meat by hand. Cut the two pounds of meat into thin slices, cut those slices into thin strips, then cut those strips into very small cubes. The end product should be pieces of meat no bigger than your pinky fingernail, or smaller. Chop the pound of fat the same way and the same size or if anything, even smaller. Mix all this with about two teaspoons of coarse salt; one tablespoon of ground black pepper; and two tablespoons of ground or crushed coriander seed (pounded in a mortar, or crushed fairly fine between two sheets of waxed paper, or bought already ground).

Now, for what we usually call "mild" or "sweet Italian" sausage, add two tablespoons fennel seed and a handful or more of chopped Italian parsley.

If you want to make "hot" Italian sausage add a scant tablespoon or less of crushed red (hot) pepper and two or three crushed cloves of garlic to the basic chopped meat mixture. (You might want to put a few tablespoons of paprika into this hot sausage, not particularly to add taste but to color it red so that, if you make both kinds, you don't wind up feeding the extra hot to the baby.)

Whichever kind you make, mix it all together and refrigerate it for at least an hour to make sure everything is blended thoroughly.

This method is, as I say, the old way of doing it. Today, I've given in and use a food processor. What I do is cut the meat into strips or cubes, but nothing as small as above, put the meat in the freezer for a few minutes until it's firm and icy but not frozen, and then chop it in the processor until it's all nice small pieces. Only half fill the machine to achieve uniform consistency. If you overfill it, you'll get some pieces ground to paste while others are still big chunks.

The third alternative for chopping the pork is to use a meat grinder. I honestly have had limited success doing this, since I think grinding tends to make the meat pastier than cutting it. Then again, all the meat grinders I've ever used were cast-offs I've picked up at garage sales. Maybe those newer-fangled models work just fine.

Now comes the good part — the tasting. After the meat has sat for a bit, take a palmful or more, make a thin patty or two, and fry it in a hot, oiled skillet. Even though, as I've said, pork these days needn't be cooked as thoroughly as in years past, there's really nothing very attractive about under-cooked sausage. Cook it through. Now let it cool and taste it. Does it need more salt? More spices? You don't want to overdo it, but you also do not want just to have fried pork either.

The meat is now ready to use as patties, or crumbled up, fried, and added to tomato sauces, or scrambled into eggs, or stuffed into "casings."

Ah ... casings. Casings are nothing more than cleaned animal intestines. Now stop it! There's nothing wrong with this. You've been eating them all your life. Every time you've bought something in "natural casings" what did you think you were getting, something made from tofu? Hot dogs, salami, sausage all make good use of this benign and fairly neutral product.

Casings come fully clean and packed in either brine or salt. The only trouble is they're not all that easy to find and they never come in small, useful amounts. These days, you'll find that you have to buy a whole "hank" of casings. This usually runs about two pounds.

Different people handle casings in different ways. When I get them home, I usually untie the hank and separate each strand. Then I find a covered plastic container big enough to hold all the casings, plus a good bit of coarse or kosher salt. I put a handful of salt in the bottom of the container, next place one or two long strands of casings on top of that, then put more salt over that, and so on, until all the casings are snug in the container, with each layer covered in salt. In the back of the fridge these salt-covered casings will keep virtually indefinitely.

To use the casings, take out a strand or two and wash them thoroughly under cool running water.
I always let water run into as well as around the casings by feeding one end of the casing over the faucet, letting the water run through and through. How many casings to use? Well, if you consider that each sausage will be about 5" long and you'll get about five or six to the pound, then have at least three feet of casings for each pound of sausage, maybe a bit more. You'll need tying and twisting room, don't forget. If you've overestimated what you'll need, no problem. Just bury the unused piece or pieces back in the salt.

If you have a modern meat grinder, take about two or three feet of casing and feed the casing over the stuffing horn on the machine. Tie a knot at the end and punch a small hole next to the knot with a knife-point or fork prong. (This is to let the meat fill the entire casing and not create an air bubble at the knot end.) Then feed the pork mixture into the casing until you near the end of the casing. With wet hands, take the long string of sausage off the horn and, starting at the knot end, twist the sausage into links every four or five inches or so. (I usually make each sausage link about the width of my hand.) Twist the first link one way, the second link the other, and so on. When you reach the end, knot off the last sausage, so that now you have a chain of sausage links twisted between each and knotted at each end. Lay the links in circles around a plate and pierce each sausage a few times in various places with a sharp fork. This will help keep the sausages from bursting as they cook.

As I said, I don't have a grinder and attachment. I have grandma's old tin funnel, whose hole end is about the width of my thumb. If your grandma left you one of these, do what I do: Feed the casing up onto the end of the funnel, then knot it and pierce it. As you work the pork into the casing it will slowly peel off the funnel, filled with meat. Keep your hands and the casing moist as you do this. When the strand comes to the end, twist it, knot it, and pierce it as above.

Fried Sausages

These are exactly what their name implies. Take as many individual sausage links as you think you'll need, usually about two per person, and in a lightly oiled pan, fry them over low heat, turning regularly, until they're done. The colder they are from the fridge, the slower you should cook them, lest the outsides burn and the insides stay raw. They're done when they have cooked through. Of course, always have an extra one cooking up to test for doneness. (Well, that's the excuse.)

Grilled Sausages

Place the sausages (again, about two per person) over a nice bed of hot coals and grill, semi-covered, until done. Semi-covered they will flare up less, char less, and smoke a bit, all of which is fine.

Now for the best part: In two separate pans, fry up a few sliced onions until lightly browned and strips of green peppers until cooked and soft. Now, take some of the soft white part out of a sandwich length of Italian bread (to make room for the sausages), put in one or two links, and cover them with onions and peppers. Salt to taste, and have the best summertime lunch in America.

American Sausage

This is not an old neighborhood recipe, but I'll include it here anyway since it's really good and we're on the topic of sausage. This is what real breakfast patties were meant to taste like, not the salty, chemically discs we get from supermarkets or fast-food joints.

Grind or chop one pound of lean pork with one-half pound pork fat. Grind it or chop it smaller than you would for Italian sausage. Add about a teaspoon of salt, a teaspoon of ground coriander, two teaspoons of freshly ground pepper, a quarter-teaspoon freshly grated nutmeg, and a handful of chopped fresh sage leaves or (actually better) two tablespoons of crumpled dried leaves. If you want hot breakfast sausage, add some red pepper flakes.

Make thin patties and fry in a lightly oiled pan. I make them thin rather than thick because I like them crispy. Fry up your eggs in the sausage fat, butter some toast, and don't tell the doctor.

Veal

Good Italian veal is a pale white pink. Veal scaloppini, cut from the leg and sliced very thin, is probably the best known of all Italian-American veal dishes.

Veal Scaloppini (al Limone)

Buy two pounds of very thinly sliced veal. Each piece should be about the size of your hand or smaller. In a large frying pan, heat a scant quarter-cup of olive oil over medium-high heat. Lightly flour two pieces of veal and fry them quickly until they're just slightly browned on each side and just cooked through. Be careful not to overcook them — because they are so thin, they cook very quickly. Set aside the pieces, lightly covered, saving any juices that collect. Cook the rest of the meat in turn, floured just before you put it in the pan.

When all the meat is done and set aside, lower the heat, add any juices that collected from the cooked veal, and add the juice of one lemon. Boil for a few seconds, scraping up and incorporating any browned bits from the pan into the sauce. If the sauce begins to cook away too quickly, add up to a quarter-cup of water or stock. The flour and oil remaining in the pan from cooking the veal should be sufficient to thicken the liquid slightly. You can also enrich the flavor by swirling in a softened nugget of unsalted butter.

Arrange the veal on a platter, lightly salt and pepper it, pour the sauce from the pan over it all, sprinkle with chopped parsley, and serve as quickly as possible with lemon wedges. A dish of fried mushrooms is perfect with this; add a good salad and you're ready for guests.

Since cooking the veal this way makes for a rather light dish, some people prefer to flour the veal, dip each piece into beaten egg, then to flour it again before frying. This process of flour – egg – flour makes for slightly more substantial pieces of meat. Cooked this way, the veal retains more of its juices, so making a sauce from the drippings is not really productive. Instead, simply squeeze half a lemon directly over the cooked veal, sprinkle with chopped parsley, and serve with lemon wedges.

Veal Scaloppini Marsala 1

Adding sweet flavors to meat is traditionally Sicilian. Here, despite the delicacy of the veal, it works just fine. Here, also, butter seems to work better than oil.

Begin by frying a half pound of mushrooms, sliced thin, in four tablespoons of butter. Cook them over medium heat until they're just done through, about five minutes. Set them aside in a bowl. Since we don't want to lose whatever juices they might still be giving off, don't put them on paper towels. Now turn to sautéing the veal.

About two pounds of thin-sliced veal will serve four to six as a main course. If the butcher didn't cut it paper-thin, pound it a bit with a wooden mallet. Dredge each piece very lightly in flour and sauté each one quickly in a few tablespoons of butter over medium-high heat. Keep adding butter, if necessary, as you cook each piece. The veal should be lightly browned and, if really thin, should need to cook for no more than 30 seconds on each side. When done, salt the pieces lightly and let them sit on a warm plate, or in a warm oven, while you finish.

With the pan still over medium-high heat, add a quarter-cup of sweet or semi-sweet marsala to the pan as well as any juice from the veal and mushrooms. Scraping the pan with a flat wooden spoon, pick up all tiny bits of meat and mushroom. Just before the marsala is on the verge of completely evaporating, remove the pan from the heat and incorporate into it a stick of soft butter.

If the veal is still warm, you can simply pour the sauce over it, spread the mushrooms on that, sprinkle it all with chopped parsley, and serve. Or, if the veal has cooled, put it in the pan with the melted butter, heat gently over medium heat, and then serve with the mushrooms on top.

Veal Scaloppini Marsala 2

This is a simpler and less heavy preparation of Veal Marsala. In either butter or oil, sauté the floured veal scallops according to the recipe above. Salt them slightly and set them aside on a warm plate or in a warm oven. If the butter has browned too much, discard it. Quickly, put one-half cup of either sweet or semi-sweet marsala in the pan and boil it down by half as you pick up the small brown bits. Add a half cup of simmering chicken stock (or veal stock, if you have it), letting the remains of the flour that was on the veal thicken the sauce slightly. Boil it down just a bit to help it thicken. As you remove the pan from the heat, add a small nugget of soft butter to help thicken and enrich the sauce as well.

Pour this over the still warm veal, sprinkle with chopped parsley and serve.

This preparation omits the mushrooms of the preceding recipe, though you may keep them in if desired.

Veal Cutlets

Cutlets are more substantial than scaloppini. Begin by lightly flouring each piece of veal, dipping them in beaten egg, then coating each piece with breadcrumbs. You can use either plain dry breadcrumbs or crumbs with a small amount of oregano, basil, salt and pepper added, or even crumbs mixed with a tablespoon or two of freshly grated Parmesan cheese. The cutlets can be breaded up to an hour or so before cooking.

To cook, heat a quarter-cup of olive oil in a large frying pan. When it's hot enough to sizzle the meat, add the cutlets to the pan without crowding or overlapping. Cook until nicely brown on each side, no longer. Set them on paper towels while the rest are cooking. When they're all done, squeeze a lemon over the top, sprinkle with chopped parsley, and serve at once.

If there were ever any cutlets left over, we'd eat them the next day in sandwiches, with catsup. It actually tastes better than it sounds.

This same procedure can be followed to make turkey or steak cutlets. Use thin-sliced, raw turkey breast meat or extra-thin minute steaks.

For all these recipes, "plain" store-bought breadcrumbs aren't bad; but I would avoid anything with additions that purport to make them "Italian Style." Making your own breadcrumbs is easy enough to do, and you can season them exactly to your taste, not someone else's. Start with a stale, dry loaf of Italian or French bread — or good, substantial stale white bread, if that's all you have — and either grate it on the finest side of a metal grater or pulverize it in the blender or food processor. Extra crumbs keep very well in a tightly sealed container or plastic bag in the freezer.

Veal Ossobuco

One would think that veal shanks, which are often more bone than meat, would be useless to the butcher and inexpensive to the buyer. Think again. Probably because of the American rage for ossobuco, veal shanks have now become a "specialty." But the strangeness of this becomes apparent when you realize that the real joy of this dish is eating the soft and delicate marrow inside the bone, while all your dinner guests leave it untouched.

Because it's the marrow and not just the meat that's important to this dish, buy only those cut pieces of veal shank that are both meaty and have a small round bone in the center filled with the marrow. That is, avoid pieces with a large, solid bone and no marrow.

Besides the marrow, the other special thing about ossobuco that makes it more than simply stewed veal with bones is the "gremolata" sprinkled on top. Traditionally, gremolata is little more than grated lemon peel and chopped parsley, sometimes with a bit of garlic. Here, however, I've taken a hint from the late Michael Field, and added a touch of orange peel to the lemon, parsley, and garlic. If you do this, you'll see how truly special ossobuco can become.

Dust six meaty veal shanks pieces in salted flour and sauté them in a quarter-cup of oil. The object here is simply to brown the meat on both cut sides to sear in the juices and flavor. You'll probably need to do this in two or even three batches. Regulate the heat so that the meat browns without burning. When browned, put each piece in a bowl to collect whatever juices might be given up. When all the shank pieces are browned, add a half-cup of white wine (or a mix of a quarter-cup lemon juice and a quarter-cup water) to the pan and over medium heat, reduce the liquid by half as you pick up all the browned bits clinging to the pan. When the liquid is reduced, add about a cup of homemade chicken or beef stock and bring it to a boil. Pour this liquid into a separate bowl.

While the shanks are cooking, dice two carrots, a large onion, two or three stalks of celery and three cloves of garlic. Aim for pieces about the size of your pinky fingernail. Put a quarter-cup of olive oil into the pan in which you sautéed the veal and cook this vegetable mix slowly until the onions become translucent and everything seems a bit limp. This should take between five and ten minutes, with regular stirring. At this point add two cups of ripe fresh tomatoes, peeled, seeded and chopped, or one cup of canned plum tomatoes, squeezed, seeded and chopped. Cook this over medium-high heat to boil off some of the water the tomatoes have given off.

Now, put this carrot-onion-celery-garlic-tomato mix in the bottom of a casserole that's big enough for all six veal shanks. Place the shanks over the vegetables, adding any liquid that accumulated in the bowl. Also add a few sprigs of parsley, a bay leaf, a few grindings of black pepper, and perhaps a teaspoon of salt. Add the wine/stock mix that you set aside, above. Remember that the amount of salt you add should take into account how salty or bland the stock you just added might be. Again, there's no "scientific" way to cook good food like this; you'll just have to rely on judgment and common sense, and on tasting everything as you go along.

Cook the casserole, covered, in a pre-heated 325 oven for approximately two hours. Be careful of two things as it cooks – first, that there's always sufficient liquid to come at least halfway up the meat and, second, that the liquid simmers but doesn't boil. Simmering will tenderize the meat; boiling will toughen it – and veal shanks are tough enough to begin with!

While everything is gently cooking, make the gremolata by removing the outer peel (the zest) of two lemons and one orange with a sharp potato peeler and chop very finely with a sharp knife. Set it all aside in a bowl. Now chop enough flat-leaf Italian parsley to make about a quarter-cup or perhaps a bit more. Add this to the peels. Now chop, as finely as you can, two cloves of garlic. Add this to the peels and the parsley and mix it together. Set this aside until the very end.

When the shanks are cooked and tender, remove them to a pre-heated serving dish. Take out the parsley sprigs and the bay leaf and spoon the chopped vegetables around the meat. If the liquid is very thin, quickly reduce it over high heat so that it's more like sauce than soup. Pour this over the meat and vegetables or set it aside in a gravy boat.

Sprinkle the gremolata over the shanks and serve it all with a side of rice or noodles and a green salad. If you put the sauce aside in a gravy boat, it can be used by each person either to moisten the rice or noodles or to put over the meat. And, please, be certain to have small teaspoons at each plate so that your guests can at least try the marrow.

Ossobuco makes an excellent fall or winter meal and is definitely "company food." One thing you might want to have for a dessert, since it's light and refreshing after so major a meal, is an orange cup filled with orange Italian ice (page 228).

Veal Parmesan

As in previous recipes, flour, egg, and flour again about two pounds of veal scallops. Cook the veal in a quarter-cup of olive oil as described above. After each piece is cooked, set it aside on a plate rather than on paper towels so as to collect and save any juices.

Mix the collected juices into about two cups of meatless tomato sauce or a sauce of fresh tomatoes and basil. Spread a half-cup of the sauce on the bottom of a small baking dish. Cover with a single layer of veal, with the pieces touching or barely overlapping. Cover with a thin layer of sauce and then with a layer of thinly sliced fresh (and only fresh) mozzarella cheese with some freshly grated parmesan lightly covering the mozzarella. Sauce the layer of cheese, add another layer of veal, of sauce, of cheese, and so forth, ending with a layer of cheese. Bake in a moderately hot (375 degrees) preheated oven for about 20 minutes, or until the cheese is melted and the sauce is slightly bubbling. Serve with a mixed green salad.

A Note on Wine

Remember the scene in The Godfather where one of the Mafia guys is cooking spaghetti sauce and pours some red wine from the bottle right into the tomatoes? I think that's one of the most chilling scenes in the whole movie. Tomato sauce is all too often acidic enough without adding more acid to it. No doubt knowing this, the guy then adds a handful of sugar to the sauce to overcome the acidity of the wine. Pitiful thing to do to a good sauce.

I know the French use wine all the time, often to advantage. But Italian cooking tends more to use lemon or a bit of vinegar when a slight bit of acidity is needed. Still, as these recipes become part of your cooking routine, you might want to try using some wine to vary the results from time to time. The Steak Pizzaiola, above, for example, could have its pan deglazed with a splash or two of red wine rather than stock. In the Veal Scaloppini, you could certainly deglaze the pan with a quarter-cup of white wine, or a wine and lemon mix. And I do have you use some white wine in the Veal Ossobuco recipe, above. Just be certain that the alcohol in the wine will have sufficient time to cook off and that the extra acidity will add to the dish rather than detract from it.

A Note on Salt

All salt is not created equal. I find most commercial salt to be good for little more than salting spaghetti water. Much of it has a harsh and metallic taste, and it imparts that taste to all the food you put it on. Coarse or Kosher salt seems somewhat better, and you can use it in any recipe that calls for salt. But there are some salts available that seem to have only "saltiness" to them, without the harshness and astringent taste of ordinary table salt. Needless to say, they are "specialty" salts, mostly sea-salt, and mostly flaked rather than finely ground, and you get soaked at the checkout counter. I definitely prefer a brand like Maldon's, both for use in a recipe or to sprinkle over a steak or hamburger — though cost drives me to use Kosher or even regular salt for things like salting water, which will be pitched in the end anyway.

Do a taste test. Get some high-grade flaked sea-salt and taste it next to both Kosher and common table salt. I think it will be a revelation.

Eggs

Eggs are also not all created equal. There was always a noticeable difference in taste between supermarket eggs and the eggs we got from the chicken market. I don't think it's just me, but eggs from factory-raised hens pecking away on fishmeal pellets and other odd goodies have a distinctly fishy taste. Sorry to say, the taste comes through worst when the egg itself is supposed to be the purest and cleanest — as in a plain poached egg on toast.

I'm sure mass-produced eggs are just as nutritious as any other; and all eggs behave pretty much the same in cooking. But you now can buy farm-raised rather than factory-raised eggs, and they're every bit as good as what you get from the old market, or by raising your own. The only trouble is, they often cost two or three as much.

So, if you're rich, forget about ever buying mass-produced supermarket eggs. But if you're like the rest of us, use mass-produced eggs for anything where the eggs are simply a binding ingredient and where their taste isn't meant to predominate. And use farm raised eggs for anything where eggs are meant, if not to star, at least to play a strong supporting role.

Peppers and Eggs

This was my father's favorite meal. When left to his own devices, he'd cook this up for breakfast, lunch, or dinner. The only difficulty in making it is deciding what kind of peppers to use — fried strips of green peppers, roasted red peppers, store-bought vinegary hot peppers? Add onions? Add garlic, too? Well, anything is possible. Let's try this:

In a pan over medium heat filmed with olive oil, cook one small onion, sliced, with one small green pepper, sliced. Cook until everything is wilted. Add to this two eggs that you've beaten separately to a froth in a small bowl. Cook until firm, but not too solid, stirring and moving it all around with a spatula or turner. Add salt and pepper to taste as it cooks.

This makes for a nice two-egg frittata for one. Eat it just plain, or in a sandwich, or even, I guess, as a side to a larger meal.

You can leave out the onions and add chopped garlic to cook with the peppers. Or you can use pickled hot peppers rinsed, drained, seeded and chopped. And if you can, get some roasted New Mexican green chilies, seed and chop them, and fry that up with the eggs. Wow.

No wonder my father liked peppers and eggs: few ingredients, easy preparation, endless variation, and really quite good.

Herbs and Eggs

When we have company coming over for breakfast or brunch, one of our favorite and least difficult meals is this mix of eggs and mozzarella with fresh herbs. Count on at least two eggs per person. Whisk them up in a bowl and add salt and pepper to taste. To this add chopped fresh basil and chopped fresh Italian parsley. How much of this you add depends on how many eggs you're cooking, but it's probably best to err on the side of minimalism, especially since you don't want the herbs to overpower the eggs. I'd start with no more than one teaspoon of chopped basil and an equal amount of chopped parsley for every two eggs. Mix these herbs with a bit of salt and pepper directly into the whipped eggs and set them in a heated pan (medium-high heat) filmed with a bit of butter or olive oil. If it looks like your taste might go for more herbs, have them ready and add them now.

Just as the eggs start to firm up at the bottom of the pan, add mozzarella cheese that you've cut into small dice and squeezed dry. (Again, in answer to the question 'How much?' The answer is, "It depends." Start with a small handful of chopped fresh mozzarella for every two eggs.) Turn and mix until the eggs are fairly firm and the cheese fairly soft.

You can vary this with the addition of other herbs — some thyme, some tarragon — but always in moderation.

Italian Sausage and Eggs

Although I mention this in passing in the recipe for sausage making, it really deserves more than just a mention. It makes for a hearty, simple breakfast as well as a fine sandwich.

Put a very thin film of oil in a frying pan over medium heat. When heated, fry up either a sliced link of mild or hot Italian sausage or the equivalent (about one-quarter cup) of loose sausage meat for every two eggs. As the sausage cooks, whisk the eggs to a froth in a bowl with a few pinches of salt. Add the eggs to the pan when the meat is cooked through. Keep folding the eggs and meat together until the eggs are just firm. Don't cook this too much past the "just firm" stage or it will become dry and rather uninteresting. Generally count on two eggs per person.

If you're making a sandwich on Italian bread, cut the bread into four- or five-inch lengths and remove the soft inside part so that the eggs can sit in the hollow between the crusts.

Leftover sausage, previously cooked, works fine here too. Simply slice or crumble it up and heat it through before adding the eggs.

Vegetables

Vegetables

I didn't know there was such a thing as a Brussels sprout until I went to college and ate it under duress. Vegetables were always spinach, canned peas, broccoli, broccoli rabe, eggplant, escarole, endive, artichokes, ciccoria, and, of course, salads. About canned peas, the less said the better. Mom would fry up some onions, add the can of peas, water and all, to the pot, heat it up and serve the mess over mashed potatoes. I loved it.

Artichokes

Artichokes were one of the few dishes we made that involved mint. Here they are with a bread and oil stuffing.

Buy the heaviest, brightest, tightest artichokes you can find. If your family is fond of them, count on one per person. With a sharp knife, cut off the stems, leaving a flat base for them to sit on. With a paring knife, peel the stems down to the white flesh and set aside.

Snap the tough leaves from the bottom quarter or even third of each artichoke and discard. Don't fret over the loss; the small bit of edible vegetable at the base of these leaves is still attached of the body of the artichoke. Next, with a sharp and heavy knife, cleanly cut off the top one-third of the artichoke and discard. Again, you've lost nothing of value. If any remaining leaves still have the little points at the ends, snip them off with a pair of scissors.

Spread open the leaves as best you can and rinse the artichokes under tepid running water or let them soak in a pot of warm water for a few minutes to be certain there's nothing hiding between the leaves.

Now you can do one of two things. Best would be to open up the center of the artichoke with your fingers to expose the little teepee of spiny purplish-green leaves. With either your fingers or a spoon remove them and remove as well the fine hairs (the "choke") under these leaves and attached to the base. Again, you're losing nothing very good. If the central purplish-green leaves refuse to budge, ignore them and pack the stuffing more between the outer leaves than in the center.

For the stuffing, mix two or three crushed and chopped cloves of garlic, some salt and pepper, a handful of chopped parsley, and a small handful of finely chopped fresh mint leaves with a cup of breadcrumbs made from day-old bread without the crusts. (You can easily make the crumbs on a grater or in a food processor. The crumbs can be small, but should not be anywhere near as fine and powdery as store-bought packaged crumbs.) Moisten this with a quarter-cup or more of olive oil. Chop up the pared stems and add them as well. (They may have discolored some while sitting, but they're perfectly fine.) This will be enough for four artichokes; increase it if you have more.

Spread this mixture evenly among all the leaves or, if you managed to remove the center leaves and choke, put the crumbs in there. Set the artichokes base-down in a casserole, add a half-cup water and a few tablespoons oil to the bottom, and cook them covered in a preheated 350° oven for about 40 minutes or over medium-low heat, on top of the stove for about 30 minutes. All these times are approximate, depending on the tenderness or toughness of the vegetable. The artichokes are ready when the bottoms of the outer leaves are tender.

Asparagus

I have lots of prejudices when it comes to asparagus. First, thick is better than thin. Second, peeled is better than unpeeled. Third, white asparagus – at least the kind you sometimes might find in an American supermarket – are rarely worth it.

Fried Asparagus

Mom mostly cooked asparagus fried. First, wash the asparagus well in a basin of warm water. Sometimes there's grit nestled in the tips. Next, with a swivel potato peeler, begin peeling the spears down from the bottom of the small leafy scales towards the base. You don't have to go all the way down on most of them since you'll snap off the hard, whitish part of each asparagus anyway. Just peel each one down into the whiter part and then let it snap wherever it seems most comfortable as you move down toward the base.

Set before yourself three plates. In the first put a handful of plain, all-purpose flour. In the second put one egg, beaten with a teaspoon of oil. Put more flour, seasoned with salt and pepper, or some very fine plain breadcrumbs, similarly seasoned, in the third plate.

Take each cleaned and peeled asparagus spear, roll it in the flour, then roll it in the egg and let any excess drip off. Finally roll it in the flour or breadcrumbs. Put the coated spears in a large frying pan with a quarter inch of olive oil over low or medium heat. Turn them repeatedly until they're cooked through the middle and brown on the outside. You may have to regulate the heat downward if they're browning too quickly. Serve hot.

Once you get the hang of it, you can try adding a few tablespoons of grated Parmesan to the last plate of flour or crumbs or incorporate the cheese into the beaten egg. Since the cheese tends to burn easily, you'll need to be extremely careful as you cook them.

Broiled Asparagus

Broiled asparagus, slightly scorched here and there, is a good way to prepare asparagus. Again, rinse the spears thoroughly to remove any stray dirt or grit. Peel each spear down toward the base. Flex each stalk and allow it to snap where the hard, woody base joins the more edible portion.

In a pan of boiling salted water cook the asparagus for four or five minutes, or until the spears are just barely done. Remove them from the water and drain well. You can do everything up to this point hours ahead of dinner.

When you're ready to begin broiling, mix a quarter cup of olive oil with a crushed clove or two of garlic in a flat pan large enough to hold the asparagus flat. Let the asparagus marinate briefly in this while the broiler heats. When the broiler is very hot, put the asparagus on a metal plate or broiler-proof dish and set it a few inches under the flames. Turn them all quickly and regularly, so that they both finish cooking and get just slightly scorched here and there.

Alternatively, you could put the marinated asparagus on a hot charcoal grill, turning rather constantly. Be forewarned, you will lose a good number of spears through the grill. But those that survive are scrumptious.

Broccoli and Broccoli Rabe

Broccoli is handsome, trim, bright, tight. Broccoli rabe, sometimes called rapini, is loose, floppy, gangly, and pale. Broccoli was always the ubiquitous, middle-class vegetable of choice. Broccoli rabe you generally had to grow in the back yard or buy from a pushcart. As kids, we always called broccoli rabe "bitter broccoli." But bitter the way a good cup of coffee is when compared to milk. Broccoli rabe may be the best vegetable in the world.

The easiest way to cook regular broccoli, not rabe, is to break it into stems and branches, wash them, peel some of the skin if the broccoli is old, and cut it all up into relatively bite-sized pieces. Boil it for about five minutes or until just tender, drain, run under cold water, drain again, and fry in olive oil and garlic.

Broccoli rabe we usually cooked a little soupier. Wash the rabe, peel the tough stems, chop it up — all of it, leaves, flowers and stems — into one- or two-inch pieces, and boil it in a few quarts of water until it's just tender. In another saucepan heat a quarter-cup of olive oil with two or three cloves of garlic, sliced. When the garlic is very pale brown and the rabe is tender, spoon the rabe and a half-cup or more of its cooking water into the oil. Be careful of splatters. Simmer this for a few minutes; add salt, pepper, and some red pepper. Then serve in bowls, maybe over a thick piece of Italian bread.

If there's any left over, heat it up the next day; it gets better with age. As a kid I loved cold, garlicky broccoli rabe sandwiches on Italian bread. I was an odd child. And broccoli rabe water is just as good to drink as ciccoria water, about which more later.

Cold Broccoli with Lemon and Oil

Wash, peel, and cut up regular broccoli, as described above. Cook it in slowly boiling water until it's just tender, no more. Rinse under cold water and allow it to cool thoroughly. Mix a quarter-cup of olive oil, one crushed clove of garlic, and the juice of half a lemon for each cup of cooked broccoli. Add this dressing to the cooked broccoli, mix thoroughly, cover with wax paper and put it in the refrigerator to serve as a cold vegetable. Don't make it more than a few hours ahead or the lemon will start to discolor the broccoli.

Eggplant

It's very important to buy the youngest eggplants you can. As eggplants get old, they not only get pulpy, but they also get bitter. Any number of cookbooks will tell you to slice and then salt your eggplant to "draw out" the bitterness. Every time I try this, I wind up with eggplant that's too salty and no less bitter. Avoid the problem by buying young eggplants, ones with taut, shiny, purple-black skins. If the skin is dull or wrinkled; or if the green prickly stem on top is dull, dark, or shriveled; or if the vegetable itself is large, fat, and soft — fuhgeddaboudit. There is simply no way to cook the bitterness out. Shape doesn't matter — they can be long, round, or squat. They just can't be old or overgrown.

Fried Eggplant 1

I generally peel my eggplant; most people I know don't. So, take your pick. To cook, first cut off and discard the green part on top. Then, after peeling or not, cut the whole eggplant into half-inch dice. Using about two tablespoons of olive oil for each medium-sized eggplant, fry the diced eggplant with a little garlic over medium-high heat until each piece is light brown on the outside and tender in the center. Since one eggplant in a frying pan will absorb all the oil you can give it, try not to use more oil than you need just to brown it. Otherwise, you'll end up with an unattractive, sodden mess. Drain the pieces on paper towels before serving.

That recipe is basic. It can be varied in several ways. Rosemary, especially fresh, is a nice addition. Two teaspoons fresh, chopped, or a half-teaspoon dried, would be enough. Or, as with zucchini, you can also add onions or tomatoes or basil. Or you could add them all, plus zucchini, and make something like a French ratatouille. If you do that, make more than you'll need and save the leftovers to eat cold the next day. That's a fabulous dish.

Fried Eggplant 2

Another good way to fry eggplant is to slice it crossways into rounds about half an inch thick, lightly flour each slice, and fry in very hot oil until golden. Don't crowd the frying pan. Drain each batch well after they come out of the oil. I've known people to add a little Parmesan cheese to the flour for added flavor; but if you do that be especially careful not to burn the slices.

Grilled Eggplant

If you have the charcoal grill on for something else, you might want to try grilling the eggplants. If they're very small, peel them, remove the tops and cut each eggplant in half, lengthwise. Make crosshatch slashes, perhaps a quarter inch deep, on both sides of each piece. Brush both sides of each piece with olive oil mixed with a clove of crushed garlic and a tablespoon or so of crushed or chopped rosemary, fresh or dried. Grill the eggplant on both sides until it's cooked through. They should look "grilled" but not burnt. Serve them very hot, as soon as they're ready.

If the eggplants are larger than two inches thick, peel and cut them into long, quarter- to half-inch thick slices. Or you could slice them into rounds, too. Again, brush each side of each slice with oil and grill as above.

Eggplant Parmesan

Buy one medium or two small eggplants. Look for firm, shiny eggplants with the freshest green caps. If you don't see eggplants that are firm, shiny, and green, make Veal Parmesan instead.

Cut off the green caps and the very bottoms and peel the eggplants. Cut them into slices about one-quarter inch thick, no less.

Make a full quart of rich tomato sauce. It can be plain, or with meatballs, or sausages, or some ground beef or veal, or simmered slowly with a piece of browned pork. It can be freshly made or taken from the freezer. Put this on to simmer just before you begin peeling and slicing the eggplants.

Now, get down a rack, two plates and one bowl. Put about a cup of flour on the first plate, whip into a froth two eggs and two tablespoons of water in the bowl, and put a cup or more of fine, unflavored breadcrumbs on the second plate. Store-bought breadcrumbs, plain, are fine. Put the sliced eggplants on the far left, put the flour next, then the eggs, then the plate of breadcrumbs, and last, on the right, the rack to hold the coated eggplant slices.

Take each slice of eggplant, one at a time, and coat it lightly on both sides with flour, holding it by the edge. Next, dip it into the egg, letting any excess drip off for a second, then coat it on both sides with the breadcrumbs. Lay it on the rack and do the next one. And the next one. And so on. (This makes a fairly substantial coating on each slice, which is why you don't want to slice the eggplant too thin — when cooked, you want to taste eggplant, not just breading.)

Every now and then check to see that the tomato sauce is simmering and not scorching.

I know this sounds like a neat assembly line kind of job, the kind of happy event that might include the whole family. Believe me, it is as conducive to family harmony as hanging wallpaper together.

When all the slices of eggplant are finished being coated, place a large heavy skillet over medium heat, and film it with inexpensive olive oil, vegetable oil, or a mixture of both. When the oil is hot enough so that each piece sizzles gently when added but doesn't burn, add the eggplant slices. Do a few at a time so as not to crowd them. When light brown on one side, turn them over and brown the other. Take each slice off as it cooks and set it aside on paper towels on a plate. Cook all the slices this way until every piece is fried up. You will almost certainly have to add more oil between batches and occasionally have to wipe out any overly browned crumbs left behind.

Grate about a cup or two of Parmesan cheese. Slice thin and pat dry about a pound of fresh mozzarella cheese. Roughly chop a handful of fresh basil leaves. Now take your sauce off the heat and spread a thin layer of sauce in a baking pan that's about 8 x 10" or 10 x 12". Put a layer of the fried eggplant on top of the thin layer of sauce, filling any large gaps between slices with any stray fried eggplant scraps. Cover this layer of eggplant with a thin layer of sauce, followed by half a handful of Parmesan, followed by a few slices of mozzarella. Sprinkle a bit of chopped basil on and about the mozzarella.

Repeat this: Eggplant, Sauce, Parmesan, Mozzarella, Basil until everything is used up and in the pan. Trust me, this part is actually easier than it sounds.

Put the pan into a preheated 325° oven for about 40 minutes. If you followed the sequence the way you were supposed to, the mozzarella on top should now be melted and maybe even very lightly browned. Take it out and let it rest for a while, maybe even up to half an hour, while you set the table, make a salad, put out whatever meat might have been cooked in the sauce, slice some bread, and open the wine.

I think this dish is even better made a day ahead and reheated in a slow oven till warmed through. It's even not half bad cold, when you go to the fridge to find something to eat at bedtime.

Fennel

Fennel is one of the few vegetables that we'd mostly eat uncooked. We didn't have it very often, usually with big, holiday dinners. And we'd have it after the meal, when the nuts and dried figs would be brought out.

It sounds like a story, but it's true — after a big meal where you can't eat another bite and you feel like an Oompa Loompa on steroids, raw fennel calms the nerves, settles the stomach, and helps get your digestion going. It has a pleasant, anise taste, a celery crispness, and a refreshing wetness all its own.

Look for fresh fennel in the vegetable aisle, (they look like bulbous celery with ferny leaves on top), cut off the green stalks and leaves and any bruised spots on the white part of the bulb, remove each frond from its base, slice each one into finger-thick sections and let them sit in ice and water until you're ready to serve it after dinner. There's always room for fennel.

You can also serve cooked fennel as a vegetable, although this was a rarity. Trim, clean, and cut the white part of the fennel bulb into lengthwise pieces. Put them into a covered casserole dish that you can use on top of the stove and simmer the fennel pieces in half a cup of chicken stock until the liquid is thick and mostly evaporated. You can add a little olive oil to this or a small piece of butter. Some chopped parsley makes this rather grayish mass look almost attractive.

Greens

Of all vegetables, greens were always the best. And the best of these — besides rapini — were ciccoria (which could be either dandelion or chicory greens), escarole, and endive. The escarole and endive you get at the market, but, back then, the dandelion and chicory greens you had to pick yourself. So, every now and then, in the spring and sometimes in the fall, we'd get a brown shopping bag, the kind with handles, and go over to the vacant lots and pick. It was best to take a knife and cut the plants just below the dirt, so the bit of root that was left would hold all the leaves together in one bunch. It didn't seem to matter much whether we picked dandelion greens or chicory greens, they both tasted the same. Besides, if the plants aren't in flower, it's almost impossible to tell the two weeds apart, and my grandmother and I never tried.

Escarole, Endive, Dandelion, and Chicory

Let's assume you've gone out into the fields, empty lots, and nearby sidewalk strips and have picked your fill of ciccoria – dandelion and chicory greens. Now what? Well, first you have to clean them.

Cleaning ciccoria is a chore. Luckily, however, success doesn't require much imagination or previous training. Pick off the dead and yellow leaves, rinse each bunch under running water, put them all in a basin or pot of cool water, and soak them, changing the water until they're clean. If you've picked a lot and can afford to be a little wasteful, discard not only the root but also most of the long stem, and use only the leafy upper two-thirds of the plant. (If you cook the whole stem, the finished product will look like a stringy mess rather than just a plain mess.) In any event, discard the little piece of root that was there only to help keep the plants together when you picked them.

Drop the leaves into a large pot of unsalted boiling water. Much to your chagrin, these leaves that you spent all morning picking will now shrink up to almost nothing. Let the greens boil for about 10 minutes and drain them in a colander, saving the water.

Taste a few. If they have a strong taste, put on a fresh pot of water and boil them again for another few minutes. Drain once more and run cold water over them. (Cold water helps set a good green color to all green vegetables. Left alone after boiling, most green vegetables try to turn a murky olive brown.) This boiling and sometimes re-boiling is what you do to all greens for a start. The completed recipes follow below.

Now, to be clear: Fifty years ago, if you wanted to cook up some dandelion greens, you had to go out to the fields and pick. But these days, with poverty food becoming an affectation of the upper classes, you can buy dandelion greens in the supermarket. I even know a place where you can buy either "organic" or "conventionally grown" dandelion greens. If the truth be known, even though they charge two arms and a leg for a few bunches, store-bought dandelion is better. It's less bitter, thicker, more substantial. And it's much easier to pick off the shelf than stooped over in a vacant lot.

Still, something's lost, even if it's not worth grinding your teeth over.

Endive (not "Belgian endive," which is a good but alien vegetable), and escarole are prepared pretty much like dandelion greens. They, too, often need a few good rinses to come clean. They tend to be milder and less bitter than field-picked greens and so usually require only one boiling.

Now, you could take these greens, drain them, and while they're still hot, add a drizzle of olive oil and a splash of vinegar and serve them just like that, but the following few ways are better.

Greens, Garlic, and Oil

This is, without doubt, one of the simplest ways of eating greens — and probably the best.

In a heavy frying pan, heat about a quarter-cup of olive oil and one or two cloves of garlic, either thinly sliced or crushed. When the garlic is just light brown, put in about two cups of the boiled drained greens and cook them, stirring, until thoroughly hot. Add salt and some red pepper, if you'd like, and serve as a simple vegetable.

Greens and Beans

This makes a somewhat heartier dish; something to have on a Saturday afternoon.

Take one can of Italian white kidney beans (cannellini) and, in a colander, rinse them thoroughly under cool water. (You could, if you want, take half a pound of dried white beans — pea, navy, white kidney, whatever — bring them to a slow boil in two quarts of water, cook them for five minutes, let them sit overnight in their cooking water, and the next day simmer them for an hour or so until they're tender. But all in all, for this, canned beans are really just as good.)

Now, in a two-quart saucepan cook two cloves of chopped garlic in a quarter-cup of olive oil until the garlic is lightly brown. Add the beans and enough fresh water— or water from the greens or chicken stock— to cover them by an inch or so. Chicken stock is the best, so use that if you have it. Let the beans simmer very slowly for about 30 minutes. Then stir in about two cups or more of cooked, drained chicory or dandelion greens and simmer it all for another half hour, stirring occasionally to keep the beans from sticking to the bottom. Add salt, pepper and red pepper as desired. When fully cooked, the beans will have disintegrated slightly, thickening the liquid. This dish is best simply served hot in a bowl over good French or Italian bread. Drink beer.

Since most of the time you won't just happen to have a few cups of chopped, cooked dandelion or chicory greens sitting around the kitchen, you can make this dish just as well with escarole or endive. Simply wash these greens well, break the leaves in half, simmer them for about 15 minutes until tender, and add them to the beans, following the recipe above.

Above all, remember that this is peasant food. Don't hesitate to use ingredients at hand, in whatever quantity you have. If you have fewer beans, or more greens; if you put in three cloves of garlic, not two; if you add an onion to the oil, or slice a carrot in with the greens, you will not die. In fact, you will feel very, very good.

Ciccoria/Broccoli Rabe Water

I know you will find this hard to believe, but the best reason not to salt the water you cook the dandelions or chicory or broccoli rabe (rapini) in is so you can drink it. Hot or cold, it's a bitter, bracing drink; a kind of tonic, a tea. I'm told by those who know that it's full of minerals, vitamins, and iron. It may even be rich in soluble fiber, which I hear virtually every day is really good for us. All I know is that grandma kept a jar of it in the fridge at all times and drank a cup every now and then. She's the one who lived till she was 96. My late mother followed in her footsteps ... she lived to be 98.

Mushrooms

I can remember only three ways we ever had mushrooms: sliced and fried, stuffed and baked, or grilled under the broiler. Fried mushrooms were ordinary fare. Grilled mushrooms make for a fine side dish or a great addition to the antipasto table. But for the holidays — Easter, Thanksgiving, or Christmas — we'd go over to the pushcarts on Union Street and buy a small, oval wooden basket of the largest white mushrooms they had and eat them baked and stuffed.

Large or small, mushrooms should be firm and unblemished, and either completely closed or open just slightly to reveal their chocolate-pink gills. They open more as they get older, and old mushrooms tend to be softer and stronger tasting. (The recipes that follow call for regular white mushrooms or the golden crimini. You could also use portabella mushrooms instead, but I find them much stronger in flavor, sometimes too strong. Try them all and judge by your own taste.)

Since mushrooms are raised on large farms in sterilized medium ("medium" is a euphemism; don't ask), to clean them just wipe them with a damp paper towel and trim the stem end with a sharp knife. If you wash them, do so quickly. But if you soak them, they'll absorb the water like a sponge and make a mess when you try to cook them.

Fried Mushrooms

Cooking garlic with mushrooms is more than just traditional. A little bit of garlic seems to bring out the flavor of mushrooms just perfectly.

Take a pound or so of fresh cleaned mushrooms and slice each one lengthwise, through cap and stem, in three or more pieces. Over relatively high heat, fry a clove of crushed garlic in two tablespoons of olive oil, being careful not to burn it in any way. When the garlic is lightly colored, add as many mushroom slices as will fit in one layer in the fry pan. Cook them, turning them constantly with a fork or wooden spatula, until they have uniformly darkened and turned limp. Don't cook them black.

Remove the first batch to a dish and add another two tablespoons of oil and another garlic clove and fry the next batch. If you put more than one layer in the pan at a time you'll get stewed rather than fried mushrooms.

You can serve fried mushrooms either as a separate vegetable, or as just something to have a small "taste" of with the meal. Or you can use them over fried meats, such as a veal scallop.

Baked Stuffed Mushrooms

Whether it's stuffed mushrooms, stuffing for a roast chicken, or baked stuffed clams, the enemy of all stuffing is water. Water makes paste. But the ally of all stuffing is oil. Use oil in moderation and your stuffing will never be soggy.

Generally speaking, allow about five good-sized mushrooms per person. Clean each mushroom as we discussed above and break off the stems. Chop all these stems coarsely. Now take one out of every five mushroom caps that are left and chop them coarsely, too.

Assuming that, in the end, you will be stuffing two dozen mushrooms, in a generous quarter cup of olive oil lightly brown two or three cloves of garlic and one onion, all finely chopped. Add the chopped mushrooms, frying them over medium heat for a few minutes until cooked.

Now, remove the pan from the heat and add a half-cup of dry breadcrumbs and a half-cup of freshly grated Parmesan. If you are using store-bought crumbs, use the plain or unflavored kind. Otherwise, just use coarsely grated crumbs made from day-old bread without the crusts. Mix all this together until the bread is thoroughly incorporated into the oil-garlic-onion-mushroom mixture. Add a good handful of chopped parsley or half a handful of chopped fresh basil. Depending on how loose or how firm you would like the stuffing to be, you can add one or two egg yolks, beaten with a teaspoon of oil, to this mix. Set it aside.

Take the mushroom caps you have left. With your hands, oil each of them with a bit of olive oil. Put them on a cookie sheet in a 375° oven for about five minutes or until they start to sweat and wilt a bit. Turn them once during this time. Remove them and let them cool.

Once cool, fill the caps evenly with spoonfuls of the mushroom and bread mixture and place them back in the 375° oven for five to ten minutes. Small mushrooms may cook more quickly; larger ones will take longer, so watch all of them carefully.

Broiled Mushrooms

This is akin to baked stuffed mushrooms, but without the stuffing. If you like portabella mushrooms, this is the perfect place to use them. Again, I think that portabellas are too strongly flavored, and I much prefer ordinary white mushrooms, or, even better, the firmer golden brown Italian ones sometimes called crimini.

Wipe clean and de-stem a dozen large, firm young mushrooms, reserving the stems for some other use. Brush them with oil, sprinkle very lightly with salt, and set them in a baking dish under the broiler, open side down, for about two minutes. The aim here is to start them cooking before we fill them.

In a small bowl, combine some very finely chopped garlic, some finely chopped Italian parsley, another light sprinkle of salt, and enough olive oil to moisten everything thoroughly. For a dozen medium-sized caps, I'd probably use one good-sized clove of garlic, a tablespoon of parsley, and two tablespoons of oil.

With tongs, turn over each mushroom and spoon into each cavity a half teaspoon, more or less, of the oil-garlic-parsley-salt mixture. Broil for another two minutes or so, being careful that the mushrooms don't collapse and the garlic doesn't burn.

Peppers

Peppers were never so much a vegetable as they were a kind of condiment. Like sauerkraut on a hotdog, fried green peppers and onions were the natural and universal addition to an Italian sausage sub. And roasted red peppers, although they're superb served with the main course as a vegetable, usually were strategically (and sometimes parsimoniously) added to the Sunday antipasto.

Hot cherry peppers are a different story altogether. A few chopped into an antipasto are fine. But, generally, they were eaten right out of the jar by men who, for some inexplicable reason, thought it worth letting it be known that they had "stomachs of iron." I guess it's an acquired taste, like putting cigarettes out in the palm of your hand or throwing salt in your eyes. However, since you don't need a recipe for spearing the hot, vinegary little demons out of the container, here's how you cook up sweet peppers. Both dishes are simply, absolutely, superb.

Peppers and Onions

One of the greatest summertime treats is to grill up some homemade Italian sausages, smothering them with onions and peppers, and eating them on good Italian bread. The recipe for homemade sausages is on page 135. Here's how to do the peppers and onions:

Buy four of the brightest, freshest, largest green bell peppers you can find. Core them, cut them in half and take out the seeds. Cut each half into lengthwise slices about a quarter-inch wide. Now, in a tablespoon or two of olive oil, sauté a chopped garlic clove or two. Add the peppers as soon as the garlic takes on any color at all, stir it all up and cover it. Make sure the flame is very low. Stir them every now and then.

Next, cut up two large onions. Do this by slicing off both ends and peeling off the onion skin and any sub-skin. Now, with a sharp knife on a steady cutting board, cut the onion in half lengthwise. Next, lay each half down flat and cut the onion crossways (not lengthwise) into what amounts to half-rings, about a quarter-inch thick or so. As you get down to the small end of the onion half you'll see that it's sometimes hard to keep the piece steady. Just turn the piece around so that your free hand is now holding the larger end of the wedge and, voilà, you can cut the whole thing easily. For more onion tricks, see, later, the paragraph imaginatively called "Onion Tricks" (page 195).

While the peppers are slowly cooking, put a tablespoon or two of olive oil in another fry pan over medium heat and, when the oil is hot enough to sizzle the onion, put the onion in, lower the heat, cover and cook.

Check and stir the peppers every now and then. Do the same for the onions. When both are limp and the onions more or less translucent, raise the heat under both pans a bit, uncover them, and let them each brown up just slightly. No promises, but if you started the peppers first and had everything sliced just right, they should both be done at the same time. If not, no worry.

Now mix both the peppers and the onions together, salt them, and put them in a serving dish to smother the sausages with. I'm telling you, you'll love it.

Roasted Red Peppers

Although most people know roasted peppers as one of the ingredients in an antipasto plate, they make a wonderful vegetable side dish with meats or grilled fish.

During the summer, when the price of sweet red peppers comes down to something approaching reason, buy a half-dozen of the brightest, reddest, blockiest ones on the market. Wash the peppers and get the charcoal grill hot. If you have some wood chips — hickory, apple, cherry — throw them on the coals. If not, don't worry. Put the whole peppers on the grill and roast them, covered, for about five minutes, depending on the intensity of the heat. Turn them often. The object is to blacken and blister the outside of each pepper without destroying the whole pepper itself.

When thoroughly charred, remove them from the grill and set them aside to cool for a few minutes. As they cool they will get rather limp.

While waiting for them to cool, mix one-quarter cup of olive oil, a quarter teaspoon of salt, and one clove of garlic, crushed, in a small bowl.

Now, with your fingers, remove as much of the blackened skin from the peppers as you can. With a sharp paring knife, cut off the top end of each pepper and slit it lengthwise. Discard the seeds. Place each pepper on a cutting board and cut them into lengthwise strips each about a half-inch wide. Perfection in this is totally unimportant.

Add the roasted pepper strips to the oil and garlic and mix well.

This can either be served right away or refrigerated for another time. If you refrigerate the peppers, bring them back to room temperature before serving.

This recipe can be increased to cover as many red peppers as you can buy. And, if you have the peppers in the refrigerator well covered with oil, they will easily keep for a few weeks.

Potatoes

Mashed potatoes were a regular at the dinner table, but we never thought of them as Italian food. More to the point are fried potatoes, boiled potatoes with olive oil, and Italian potato salad.

Fried Potatoes

Depending on whether you fry the potatoes in olive oil or animal fat, the taste will be different. Both are wonderful.

Peel and wash russet (baking) potatoes, about one medium sized potato per person. Slice them evenly into rounds about a quarter-inch thick. Heat either a generous half inch of olive oil or the same amount of animal fat (lard, bacon fat, chicken, duck, or – best of all – goose grease) in a large frying pan. Set the heat at medium high. When the oil or grease is very hot, slide in the potatoes, moving them around with a spatula or turner so they brown evenly, without burning and without the oil smoking. You may have to do this in two batches as not to crowd the pan too much.

When brown on the outside and tender within, drain them on paper towels and dust them with coarse salt. Serve quickly.

Boiled Potatoes with Olive Oil

This may be the simplest way of eating potatoes other than raw. Estimating about three small or one large boiling potato per person, scrub the outside of the potatoes and put them in a large pot of rapidly boiling, salted water. Depending on their size, it will take at least 20 minutes, probably more, for them to cook through. They're done when a sharp meat fork or knifepoint goes in easily.

Remove them from the heat, and slice or cut them into small wedges. Pour over the warm potatoes enough good olive oil into which you've crushed one small clove of garlic. Coat each piece well. Sprinkle chopped Italian parsley over it all, dust it with coarse salt, and serve it while still warm.

Italian Potato Salad

Cook boiling potatoes exactly as directed for Boiled Potatoes with Olive Oil, above. Once removed from the heat and peeled, cut each potato into slices about one-quarter inch thick. Have ready a quarter-cup red wine vinegar mixed with an equal amount of olive oil. Pour this over the potatoes while they're still hot. The object is to have the potatoes absorb the vinegar while the oil gently coats them. Taste. If they could use more vinegar, add it by teaspoons and continue to mix gently. When the potatoes are just piquant enough without being too sour, salt carefully and add a generous handful or two of chopped scallions, including part of their green tops. Serve warm.

Salads

Lettuce Salad

Growing up, salad was invariably iceberg lettuce with vinegar, oil, and salt. Back then, iceberg and Romaine were pretty much all there was, though now there's leaf and red-tipped and bibb and butter lettuces, all of which are very good. Whatever kind of lettuce you choose, all it needs for a dressing is your best, fruitiest olive oil used liberally, a splash of red-wine vinegar, used sparingly, and a sprinkling of salt. You can mix these together in a little bowl and spread it over washed and impeccably dried and broken leaves of lettuce. Or, which might be more traditional, you can put the oil on the leaves in a salad bowl, then sprinkle on some vinegar then dust it lightly with coarse salt.

You can vary this in several ways, though this simple Italian dressing should always be your mainstay. First, you can substitute lemon juice for vinegar. It's a different taste — a taste that always seems to me to be fresh and summery — and a reasonable substitute for vinegar now and then. You can also use balsamic vinegar instead of red-wine vinegar. Balsamic is sweeter and less acetic than wine vinegar, with a taste that sometimes can only be described as luscious. It's fairly new to America, but if we had had it back then (and could have afforded it) we would definitely have used it. Third, it's okay, every now and then, to crush a small clove of garlic into the dressing, mixing it in well before you pour the dressing over the greens. Fourth, occasionally, especially with Romaine lettuce, it's nice to grate some Parmesan cheese on the coarse or shredding blade of your grater over the salad after you've added the dressing.

All you need to remember are a few simple rules. First, do not drown the salad in dressing. This isn't a soup. Second, go easy on the vinegar. Too much and all you'll taste is vinegar. If your oil is fragrant, you want that to be the dominant note. Third, read the ingredients on the bottled "salad dressing" you have in the fridge, then throw it away.

Mixed Green Salad

Although an all-lettuce salad might be the most traditional, there's absolutely no reason not to vary it with the addition of other greens. To my taste, the best of these salads still are made with lettuce, usually a leaf lettuce or a smooth butter lettuce, as the base.

To a bowlful of washed and dried lettuce add any or all of the following — curly or Belgian endive leaves, torn radicchio leaves, a bit of shredded carrot, tomato wedges, torn arugula. Take care, however, with the arugula. When it's mild, it's wonderful — pungent, earthy, peppery. When it's strong it will overpower everything else in the salad.

Mix this with a dressing of oil and either wine vinegar or lemon.

Tomato Salad

The tomato salad listed in the chapter on Antipasti is perfect as a summer salad served with or after meals.

Salad with Gorgonzola

Obviously, a variation – and improvement – on "blue cheese dressing." Take a small nugget of Gorgonzola cheese and mash it in a bowl with a few tablespoons of good olive oil. Keep adding oil till you have enough to lightly dress the salad you've put together. Add a splash or two of either balsamic or red-wine vinegar, mix thoroughly and dress the salad. There may be sufficient salt in the cheese that you don't need any more.

Pear and Gorgonzola

This is a variation on a kind of salad we'd sometimes have after meals on feast days. First, buy only the most perfectly ripe, firm, fragrant pears, one per person. Peel each pear, core and slice it into thin wedges. Arrange these pear slices on individual lettuce leaves on individual plates. Mix your best olive oil with some balsamic vinegar, perhaps in a four- or five-to-one ratio of oil to vinegar. Crumble a few small pieces of Gorgonzola or

Roquefort over each plate of pears. Break up a few walnut halves over the pears and cheese. Finally, drizzle the oil and balsamic over the walnuts, cheese, and pears, and serve.

Often, rather than walnut halves, we would gently toast some pignoli nuts (shelled pine nuts) in a dry frying pan over medium heat until they just started to take on a light brown color. Sprinkle them on the salad and dress with the oil and balsamic.

This is usually served after the main course, combining a salad with a hint of dessert. But it could also make a wonderful first course, especially if followed by a light one-dish dinner, something like a clam or mussel soup.

Spinach and Chard

Spinach and chard are related, members of the beet family. Which means that you can also cook beet greens as you might spinach and chard, and vice versa.

Back in the day, spinach was always notoriously gritty. Now one can find "triple-washed baby spinach leaves" hermetically sealed in plastic pouches. I'd like to be dismissive of such new-fangledness, but that would be unnecessarily obnoxious.

If you do buy or grow bulk not bagged greens, be certain to wash them well. Un-prewashed leafy greens of any kind need a fair amount of cleaning. Wash them all thoroughly in a basin in a few changes of water. Contrary to common opinion, the water you wash the greens in doesn't need to be ice cold. Lukewarm water does a better job and is much easier on your hands. (I once put a bushel of spinach in the washing machine on gentle cycle, no soap. Only do this if you're not married.)

Sautéed Spinach

The easiest and best way to cook young and tender spinach is simply to wash it, shake it dry, and sauté it in a bit of olive oil in which some sliced garlic has just started to turn golden. Since the spinach, if it's truly young and tender, needs only to be wilted, not cooked, this takes just a few seconds. Be aware that spinach cooks down to a fraction of what you thought you bought, so buy plenty. A few drops of your best olive oil plus salt and pepper are all that's needed to complete this.

Older spinach — larger leaves, tougher stems — as well as chard, turnip, and beet greens generally need a pre-cooking in some boiling, salted water for a minute or two before being sautéed in the oil and garlic. In this case, wash the greens well, discard any exceptionally tough stems, trim off any discolored parts, chop them roughly, and plunge them into boiling salted water for a few minutes. Run them under cold water to set the color, then proceed with the frying in oil.

Chard with Parmesan

Chard (often called Swiss chard, though it's perfectly at home in an Italian kitchen) can be simply fixed by cutting it all – stems and leaves – into two inch pieces, boiling until just cooked, draining it well, drizzling some very fragrant olive oil over it, and mixing in a handful or two of grated Parmesan.

Zucchini and Yellow Squash

To listen to the old ladies at the market you'd swear that the greatest agricultural feat since the planting of the Garden of Eden was the harvesting of immense zucchini. When they found truly world-class zucchini – the kind that could be used for softball bats – they'd invoke the Madonna to come witness the sight. Then, after the required oohing and aahing was over, they'd take half a dozen of the smallest zucchini on the cart and leave the exhibition-size vegetables for the Americans to buy. Do the same: don't buy big zucchini. They're tough, watery, and tasteless all at the same time. And although most Italians seem to prefer zucchini to yellow summer squash, both are similar and can be cooked the same way.

Fried Zucchini

Wash about four six-inch zucchini or yellow summer squash well under running water. Be somewhat thorough, since the skins can be gritty. Trim off each end.

Without peeling, slice each crossways into quarter inch thick circles. Or cut each one lengthwise, then each piece lengthwise again, then in half sideways, so that you have triangular sticks each about three inches long. Peel and slice or dice an onion.

In two tablespoons of olive oil, cook one clove of crushed garlic until golden. Add the onions and cook, stirring occasionally, until the onions are limp and translucent. Add the zucchini and cook until tender. Salt and pepper as desired. Serve with half a handful of chopped Italian parsley sprinkled over the top.

If you happen to have a tomato or two around, and some fresh basil, all the better. Core and squeeze the seeds out of the tomato, chop it roughly, and add put it in with the onions when you add the zucchini. As you're cooking and stirring, add four or five basil leaves, chopped.

Zucchini Blossoms

The Italian family down the block from us grew dozens of zucchini plants in the vacant lot we euphemistically called the backyard. (I know, we were all Italians. But these people had just come from Italy; they were real Italians.) Occasionally, late in the summer, the mother would come out on the sidewalk with a platter of fried zucchini blossoms. We'd all stop playing whatever variation of stoopball or Chinese handball we had invented for the day and grab a handful of cooked flowers. It wasn't until 30 years later that a few establishments decided that they could sell "sautéed squash blossoms" as exotic, expensive appetizers. Back then it was just something to eat so you wouldn't starve before dinner. Besides, if you didn't fry them up, all those millions of blossoms (mostly male, without hope of direct offspring) would just go to waste.

Chances are good you'll not find zucchini blossoms at Kroger's. So, you'll just have to plant lots of zucchini in the backyard. Pick a dozen or more male flowers. (The female flowers have a budding squash behind them; males only have a stem.) The flowers can be picked on the day they're opening, the day before, or the day after.

Beat an egg with two tablespoons of water, mixing until it's thoroughly blended. Put a small handful of flour on two separate plates, placing one to the left and the other to the right of the watered-down egg. Holding each flower by its stem, dust each one in the first dish of flour, dip them next in the egg (letting the excess egg drip off), then coat them with the flour in the second dish.

Meanwhile, heat about a quarter inch of olive oil in a pan. When the oil reaches a moderately high temperature — hot enough to cook each flower in a minute or so but not so hot as to burn them — place a few in the pan without crowding. Turn them over as they become golden brown, then drain them on paper towels. Sprinkle with salt and eat while they are still hot.

A few variations are, as always, possible. You could, for instance, do flour, egg and breadcrumbs rather than flour, egg and flour. You could grate some Parmesan cheese into the egg (maybe a scant quarter-cup), mixing it in well. Or you could open up each flower and insert a thin sliver — thinner than your pinkie — of drained and lightly salted mozzarella cheese. Twist the end closed, then flour, egg, etc.

One word of caution: If the flowers weren't clean enough and you felt the need to rinse them off, make sure they are completely dry inside and out before you fry them. Water drops in hot oil cause unpleasant, small explosions and bad little burns.

Onion Tricks

Onions are a fairly common ingredient in Italian cooking. But my guess is — since they're round, sometimes surprisingly resilient, and always need peeling — that more amateur chefs cut themselves working with onions than with almost anything else.

The first problem is dull knives. Dull knives slide off the material to be cut and onto you. Never cut anything harder than soft butter with anything other than a high-quality, very sharp kitchen knife. Regularly sharpen your knives with a sharpener and even more often hone them on a steel. If you don't have a steel, you can hone knives passably well by sliding their edges up and down against each other. But, now to onions.

In one of the recipes above we mentioned how to cut onions into half-rings — On a steady cutting board, carefully slice off both ends of the onion. Cut a slit lengthwise down the onion from one end to the other, going through both the outer, papery skin and the first layer of onion flesh. Peel this all away.

Now, cut the onion in half lengthwise. Laying each half down flat, cut the onion crossways (not length-wise) into half-rings. You'll see, as you get down to the small end of the onion half, that it's sometimes hard to keep the piece steady. Just turn the piece around so that your free hand is now holding the larger end of the wedge and, voilà, you can cut the whole thing easily. The trick is always, first, to work with the onion flat on the cutting board; and second, always to be grasping the onion by the widest end possible.

To dice an onion, follow the same initial steps — Cut off the ends, slit it, peel it, and slice it lengthwise. Now, with each half lying flat, cut one half again in half with a crossway cut in the middle. Do the same to the other piece. You now have four wedge-pieces, all sitting squarely on the board. Beginning at the flat end of each wedge, cut the onion length-wise as thick as you want each diced piece. Then cut across each of these slices. You now have, without any other cutting, diced onions.

Hints on Garlic

When my wife-to-be and I were courting, she thought she'd impress me by making lasagna. So, she borrowed a recipe from one of her Italian neighbors. It called for two cloves of garlic cooked into the tomato sauce. Well, being Irish and not Italian, she didn't know "clove" from "head." So, I got lasagna with two heads of garlic in it, maybe about 30 cloves or so. Know what? It was great.

All this only goes to prove that garlic is a food, not a spice or herb. (The French have a wonderful dish called Chicken with Forty Cloves of Garlic. This is greatly to their credit.)

So, cloves are the individual pieces; a head of garlic is the whole thing. Now, that was fairly easy. Easy, too, is buying garlic at the store. Look for fat, firm, full heads. They can be pure white or purple streaked, depending on the variety. Needless to say, avoid heads that are light weight (which mean they're probably dried out) or bruised or blemished in any way.

Very few Italian recipes call for unpeeled garlic cloves. But peeling them is easy: with a paring knife just cut off the little flat end where the clove attaches itself to the head and peel the papery skin down and away. There are also small rubber tubes (they look like cannoli) that you put individual cloves in and roll back and forth on the countertop. They work like a charm, for no apparent reason.

Garlic can be used whole, sliced, chopped, mashed or crushed, depending on the dish being made. Garlic presses work fine for crushed garlic, though usually it's easier just to put the cloves on a cutting board, cut them lengthwise a few times, then slice them across the cuts into tiny pieces. When cooking garlic, it doesn't make all that much difference whether you've mashed, sliced, or crushed it. When eating it raw (let's say, with oil over a tomato salad), try to mince or chop the cloves as finely as you can.

Please, please, do not use commercial garlic powder or garlic salt. Fresh garlic is so tasty, and so easy to use. Because they can readily go rancid, there's often little that can ruin a good dish faster than onion or garlic powder, especially if you keep the jar in the kitchen over the stove. I've always thought that garlic powder was invented for people who really don't like garlic — and it will reconfirm their prejudice every time they use it.

Growing Garlic

Finally, a note on growing your own garlic. Most vegetables you'd set out in the spring. Not so with garlic. In winter they like to set down roots and transform their meager cloves into plump garlic heads. So, take a big head of fresh garlic, break it into individual cloves, and when the first snow of early winter falls, go out into the garden where the soil is loose and deep, and poke holes six inches down into the soil. Space these holes six or so inches apart and drop in the cloves, pointy side up. Cover, water, and wait, serenely, all through the winter. Soon, in earliest spring, their green shoots will poke up through the cracking dirt. Give them water and sun and, by summer, you will have an abundance of new, subterranean heads of garlic all your own. When the leaves start to die down, lift each garlic head out with a garden fork, let them dry in a shady spot for a few days, then braid them up. Then give some to your best friends, just to show off.

Calzones, Pizzas, and Pies

Pizzas and Calzone

Pizzas

'Tis as sad as it is true that one cannot make a real New York thin crust pizzeria-style pizza at home, ever. From what I'm told, it's not the dough, or the swirling in the air, or the sauce — all that could be copied. It's in the incredibly hot, often coal-fired, ovens that can't be duplicated by any home stove.

So, it's probably best not to try. Still, a good (but different) breadier "Sicilian-style" pizza can be made quite easily at home.

First, for the dough: Combine one-and-a-quarter cup of flour and a half-teaspoon salt in a mixing bowl. In a smaller bowl mix together two tablespoons of olive oil, one-half cup of warm water, a teaspoon of sugar and a package of active dry yeast. The water should be warm to the touch, not hot, since water that's too warm (over 125° or so) can kill the yeast rather than activate it.

After the yeast mixture has sat for a few minutes, stir it up and add it to the flour bowl. Mix everything with your hands or a wooden spoon, put the dough on a lightly floured countertop, and knead it with floured hands for a minute or two. The dough will (or should) still be slightly sticky. Form it into a ball and put it in a lightly oiled bowl, covered with a cloth, until it rises to double its original bulk, about 30–40 minutes.

While the dough rises, preheat the oven to 450° and make the sauce. Now, sauces can be anything you'd like, so long as they're tomato. If you want to make a tomato sauce expressly for your homemade pizza, try this: In a saucepan, very lightly brown two cloves of chopped or crushed garlic in a tablespoon or two of olive oil. Add one small can of tomato paste with enough water to rinse off the sides of the can and thin the paste just slightly. Tomato paste used this way gives the pizza a richer, sweeter tomato taste which I've always associated with pizza sauce. Cook this for about five minutes, then add a can of crushed or chopped tomatoes. Oregano is traditional in pizza sauce, so if you like the flavor (I don't, particularly) add a half teaspoon or so, dried. Let this simmer gently for about a half-hour.

When the dough has doubled, punch it down and turn it out onto a floured surface. Roll the dough out to a circle no more than a foot across or a rectangle that's nearly equivalent. (Or, if you think you're good at it, pull it, stretch it and toss it. Just remember – no holes, no dropping it on the floor.) Leave the dough around the edges about twice as thick as the dough in the center. Put the dough on a lightly oiled cookie sheet, cover with a cloth, and let it rest for fifteen minutes. You want the dough to rise a bit before you sauce and bake it. Now, spoon and spread the sauce on the dough, leaving the raised edges uncovered. (You will have some sauce left over. It freezes perfectly well for next time.) Snip a small handful of fresh basil over the sauce. Put about a half pound of sliced fresh mozzarella cheese evenly over the basiled sauce and sprinkle a half-cup (more or less) of Parmesan cheese on that.

Put the cookie sheet with its pizza in the oven for 12 to 15 minutes, watching that the cheese on top doesn't burn. If you own one of those oven tiles made especially for baking bread, pre-heat it in the oven and cook the pizza on that rather than on a cookie sheet.

When it's done, remove the pizza from the oven, score it into eight pieces like they do at Domino's, and serve it hot.

Variations? Sure. Thin slices of pepperoni (which I personally can't stand) or crumbled and partly cooked mild Italian sausage (which I love) can go on top of the cheese. So can pieces of anchovies, rinsed and dried. Or a cup of sautéed mushrooms. Or fried onions and peppers. Actually, most anything can go and have a claim to authenticity, except for pineapple chunks. (In the summer don't even make a sauce — just use thinly sliced plum tomatoes, basil, garlic and olive oil, either simply plain or with shredded mozzarella sprinkled over it.)

Calzone

A calzone is a baked pocket of pizza dough with the filling tucked away inside. I loved them so much as a kid that I would walk home from school partly to save the nickel bus fare but mostly to go past the pizzeria and get a hot calzone, wrapped in brown paper, to tide me over on the last leg of the walk.

Make a pizza dough exactly as described in the pizza recipe, above. Then, roll it out into a circle a foot in diameter. Let the dough rest for 10 or 15 minutes, covered with a cloth. Then, on one half of the dough, heavily spread a half pound of ricotta cheese mixed thoroughly with one beaten egg, a handful of chopped Italian parsley or some snipped fresh basil, and some salt and pepper. Sometimes I put grated Parmesan, about half a cup, into the ricotta; sometimes I don't. Over this put a quarter pound of sliced fresh mozzarella. On top of this mound of cheeses put two or three very thin slices of prosciutto. Fold the naked half of the dough over the filled half and crimp the edges together. A bit of water will help the two edges stick better. (Or you can hold out a few spoonfuls of the beaten egg and use it both to help seal the edges and also as a light wash to glaze the top of the calzone.) You now have a half-moon of dough encasing a cheese-egg-meat mixture. With a fork, punch a few holes in the top. Let the calzone sit for another five minutes so the dough can gather its wits about itself and begin a small rise. Put the calzone on an oiled cookie sheet and bake it for about 45 minutes in a preheated 350° oven. Serve it hot, perhaps with a green salad.

If you'd like, you can cut the ball of dough in half, divide the filling, and make two small rather than one large calzone. The timing is still approximately the same.

In Sicily and in many places in America it seems traditional to put either slices of fresh tomatoes or tomato sauce in with the cheese or serve it with a tomato sauce "topping." Personally, I think this detracts from the simple greatness of a calzone; but try it that way and see if it suits your taste.

Easter Pie

This is the traditional Easter Pie of both Naples and New York. The cookbooks all refer to it as "Pizza Rustica." Along with homemade sausages, cannoli, lemon ice, and lasagna, this was at the heart of what it meant to grow up Italian-American in the City.

For the crust, the "recipe" (such as it was) that my mother's mother used was a yeasted bread dough — the same dough we saw in either the pizza or the calzone recipe, just above. Now, there's no reason not to do it that way, except for the fact that it makes for a very bready crust — a crust that can get rather soggy the longer it sits. But since this pie is little more than a kind of Italian quiche, there's no reason not to use a flakier and more delicate quiche-like crust.

So, here's a fairly standard recipe for a quiche-like crust, so long as you realize that there are, on the internet, an uncountable number of variations to choose from besides this one.

Have at the ready a 9" deep dish pie pan. Preheat your oven to 350 degrees. Then, using the food processor, pulse 2 ½ cups all-purpose flour with ½ teaspoon salt and 1 teaspoon baking powder. (Baking powder seems to help make the dough both firmer and flakier at the same time.)

Now, add 12 tablespoons (3/4 cup) of very cold unsalted butter, cut into small cubes, or a mix of butter and firm lard. Pulse until the mixture resembles corn meal or breadcrumbs. Add 1/3 cup ice water. Pulse again until the dough forms.

Remove the dough from the processor and let it sit, wrapped in waxed paper in the fridge as you make the filling.

In a bowl mix two pounds ricotta cheese, a half-pound of fresh mozzarella cheese, cut into either strips or cubes, a quarter-cup or more grated Parmesan cheese, one-half cup chopped Italian parsley, a half teaspoon of salt, a teaspoon of freshly ground black pepper, a three quarters of a pound of thinly sliced prosciutto cut into bite-sized pieces, and four eggs beaten with a one or two tablespoons cream or milk. (If you wish, it's quite traditional to add salami, mortadella, or cooked sausage meat. I tend not to, since I so much love the taste of the prosciutto; but you certainly can, if you want. Just cut back on the prosciutto.)

Now, return to the dough. Turn it out onto a floured countertop and cut it into two pieces, one roughly twice as big as the other. Roll the larger piece into a circle that will fill your 9" pie dish and hang one inch over the edge. Try not to stretch the dough. Fill the lined dish with the cheese and meat filling. Now, roll out the remaining piece of dough for a top crust. Lay it on top of the filling, cutting it so that it overhangs by one inch. Fold and crimp the bottom and top crusts together into a fluted edge.

Beat one egg yolk with one tablespoon of water or milk and brush it over the top. Decorate the top crust with scraps of dough, if desired. (I like to cut the dough into small daisies or Easter lilies, just because they're easy enough to match my limited artistic ability.) Cut four or five steam vents into the top crust. (Try not to get the egg glaze into the vents or they might seal up and the whole top lift off. Don't laugh; it happens.) Or, if you're adept at making a true lattice top, that would be perfect.

Bake the pie in the preheated 350° oven for one hour, or until the top is nicely browned. Remove from the oven and let the pie sit for a few hours. Serve the pie cool but unrefrigerated. The pie can be kept unrefrigerated for up to a day. Refrigerate it if it must be kept longer than that, though the longer you hold it the soggier the bottom crust might become.

Spinach Pie

Make your dough exactly as in the preceding recipe for Easter Pie and line the 9" pie plate with the bottom crust. Into this you will simply put spinach or chard or beet greens (or a combination of them) sautéed in olive oil with garlic and some hot red pepper flakes. Refer to the recipe for sautéed spinach in the chapter on Vegetables. Just remember to make much more than you think you'll need because these greens cook down very far. (If, even after this friendly warning, you find yourself with not enough spinach filling, drop down to an 8" pie plate.)

As in the recipe for Easter Pie, cover the spinach with the top crust, seal it, vent it, glaze it, and bake it accordingly. Let it sit a bit before slicing and serve it just warm, not hot.

"Italian Pancakes"

An argument could be made that something like this has no place in a good cookbook. On the other hand, these were the first things I ever cooked as a child without adult supervision, and I've liked them ever since.

To be brutally honest, "Italian Pancakes" is the name we euphemistically used for fried school paste. That is, flour and water, salt and pepper, mixed into a thickish batter, fried in a decent amount of hot fat and salted when done. That's it. The very height, or depth, of poverty food.

Eat them hot and they're just fine ... or, at least, they fill you up.

Interestingly, you can vary the recipe and work your way up to regular American pancakes. Substituting milk for water makes them cakier; adding an egg, firmer; adding baking powder and soda, lighter. Put maple syrup and butter on these new-fangled cakes and you've gone from fried paste to flapjacks, from the Old World to the New, from poverty to luxury. Or something like that.

Desserts

Desserts

Pastries

All cookies, all pastry, came from the pastry store. On Sunday, we would cross the highway and go up to Union Street, where there were the pushcarts, the pastry stores, and the place where they killed chickens. Since we had dinner early every Sunday, anise cookies, sfogliatelli, pignoli cookies, or cannoli were what we'd have later in the evening with coffee. Sfogliatelli were my hands-down favorite, but they can't easily be made at home. But, if you're somewhat adept at deep fat frying, cannoli isn't that hard. Let's start there:

Cannoli

At the supermarket, you can now buy already prepared cannoli shells, ready for filling. I honestly don't have a good feel for them. In order to withstand the rigors of shipping and handling, they tend to be thick and hard rather than light and crisp. Homemade cannoli shells simply are much better.

Cannoli Shells

Cannoli shells are deep-fried pastries formed around cylindrical metal tubes. The tubes can be purchased at almost any good kitchen store. Six is a convenient number to have.

To make the dough, combine two-and-a-half cups all-purpose flour with two tablespoons butter or lard and one tablespoon sugar. Mix this together either in a food processor or with a fork in a bowl. When the flour is thoroughly mixed and grainy, slowly add one scant cup of cold water. A sweet wine such as Marsala can substitute for up to half of the water. This should make a fairly stiff dough. Break it into three or four pieces and let them sit in the refrigerator for at least an hour.

Take each piece and roll it out very thinly, about one-eight of an inch thick or thinner. Cut the rolled out dough into squares two to four inches on a side. Lightly oil the outside of each cannoli tube. Starting with the tube centered at a point of the square, roll the dough loosely around the metal tube, sealing the end point down with a dab of water. (If you wrap them too tight, you'll have a harder time removing them from the tubes.)

Fry two or three at a time in deep fat (350°) until golden brown. Let the shells drain and cool for a minute or two, then carefully, with paper towels, pull the metal tube out. Put the shells on a wire rack to cool as you make the rest. The shells must be thoroughly cool and dry before filling. This recipe will make about 24 large shells and up to 48 minis.

Using a sweet wine for part of the water gives a nice taste to the shells, and I usually add it. But it is not imperative to add alcohol to this dough — an all-water dough also makes for crisp shells that serve simply as delicate vehicles for the sweet filling. Some books say that wine is needed to give the shells their characteristic bubbly bumpiness, but it's not true. Made just with water your shells will be more than bumpy enough.

Finally, you can re-roll any dough scraps to make even more cannoli shells, or you can fry the pieces along-side the cannoli, drain them separately, and dust them heavily with powdered sugar, to give you something to eat while you slave over the hot fat.

Cannoli Filling

There are two kinds of filling for cannoli: pastry cream and ricotta cheese. Many pastry stores carry the cream-filled type, but we always preferred ricotta. To fill all the shells you've just made you will need three pounds of ricotta. (This dessert may be delicate, but it's not light.) Stir in a half-cup of sugar. Then, with a sharp knife, roughly chop one-half cup of chocolate chips and add it to the ricotta. Rinse six ounces of store-bought candied fruit — orange, citron, or lemon — under running water. Drain them, chop them coarsely, and add them to the ricotta as well. If you want to be fancy, you can let the fruit rest for a few minutes in a quarter cup of Grand Marnier, rum, or some other alcohol, then add it and the liquor to the cheese. If you don't use any liquor, you may add a half teaspoon of vanilla extract or (my favorite) a teaspoon of orange blossom water. Mix thoroughly. Taste for sweetness. (If you use your own homemade candied peel (see page 226), there's no reason to rinse the pieces.)

Fill the shells using a teaspoon, or, better, use a pastry tube with a wide opening. Arrange the filled shells on a platter, dusting them lightly with powdered sugar and, if desired, cinnamon. If you have shelled pistachios, chop a handful or two and dip the cannoli ends in the nuts.

Zeppole

Zeppole, which, I'm told, were named after the zeppelins of the last century, are little more than fried dough dusted with confectioner's sugar. They're a mainstay of every Italian festival and street fair.

In one cup of lukewarm water dissolve a teaspoon of sugar and one package of active dry yeast. Mix two cups of flour in a bowl with one tablespoon of sugar and a half teaspoon of salt. When the yeast has begun to foam up, add it to the bowl with the flour, mix it with a wooden spoon, turn it out onto a floured surface and, with floured hands, knead the dough for about two minutes. The dough should still be fairly soft and sticky when you're done. Put it in an oiled bowl, roll it around till it's lightly coated, cover with a cloth, and set it aside until it doubles in bulk, perhaps in a half-hour.

When the dough is near double, fill a wide and deep saucepan with at least three inches of oil or lard. More is better than less. Heat the oil to about 350°, or until a small piece of dough puffs and browns fairly quickly, without either burning or getting greasy.

With oiled hands pull a piece of golf-ball sized dough off the now-doubled mass of dough, pat it down to about the size of your palm, and gently drop it into the hot oil. When it's brown on one side, turn it over with a long-handled fork or spoon to cook on the other side, then remove it to a plate lined with paper towels. When they're all fried and have begun to cool, dust them all fairly heavily with confectioner's sugar and, if you'd like, some powdered cinnamon. This recipe makes about 15 zeppole.

Fried Bows

Oddly enough, this is little more than sweetened fried egg pasta. They're great fun during the holidays.

In a large bowl, mix two cups of all-purpose flour with four beaten eggs, a large pinch of salt, a tablespoon of oil, two teaspoons of sugar and two tablespoons of a liquid like sweet Marsala, port, or dark rum. With either a fork or your hands mix this together, form it into a ball and, on a well-floured surface, knead the dough for about 10 minutes. Roll it back into a ball, put it in an oiled bowl, and roll it around to coat it with some of the oil in the bowl. Cover it with a damp cloth and let it rest for an hour or so.

After it has rested, cut the dough into quarters and roll each one out on a lightly floured surface until you have a paper-thin sheet. Set a deep frying pan over medium-high heat and melt sufficient lard or shortening or oil to give you a depth of at least one inch. Cut the dough into strips about 7" long and a one-half inch wide. Tie the strips into very loose knots and fry them on both sides until golden. Remove from the oil and drain on lots of paper towels.

As with all frying, the oil should be hot enough so that the bows cook quickly, without either sogging up or burning. Keep regulating the heat as you cook.

When you're ready to serve them, sprinkle them heavily with confectioner's sugar.

Aunt Margaret's Ricotta Pie

For this you will need an eight- or nine-inch springform pan.

Take two level cups unsifted flour and add a teaspoon of sugar and a half teaspoon of salt. Then cut in one cup of cold butter or one cup of cold butter and lard mixed. You can do this with a pastry cutter or with a wide tined fork or, best of all, do it in a food processor. When well mixed, it should be grainy, not smooth.

To this add two lightly beaten egg yolks and two tablespoons ice-cold water. Shape the mass into a ball and chill it in the refrigerator for half an hour or so. Set aside about a quarter of the total for a lattice top and chill that as well.

Now flour a board or counter-top and a rolling pin. The dough will and should be somewhat soft. Roll out the dough and line the interior of the springform pan. Patch any holes. Don't fret if the dough doesn't rise exactly to the top of the pan — neither will the filling.

For the filling start by mixing three cups ricotta cheese (about one-and-a-half pounds) with one-quarter cup flour, two tablespoons grated orange peel, one tablespoon grated lemon peel, one tablespoon vanilla extract (please — use the real thing, not "imitation flavor" vanilla), and two pinches of salt.

In another bowl, beat four eggs until light and foamy. Beat into these eggs one cup of sugar.

Now add the sugar-egg mixture to the ricotta cheese mixture and blend until smooth. Pour the filling into the lined springform pan. Roll out the saved pastry dough and, with a serrated-edge pastry cutter, cut the dough into inch wide, ten-inch-long strips. Criss-cross the top of the pie with these strips to make a neat lattice.

Place the pie in a pre-heated 350° oven and bake for 50–60 minutes. The aim is to come out with a moist (not dry, not runny) cheesecake. After about 45 minutes, test the center of the cake with a cake-tester or broom straw.

If the tester comes out wet, the cake is still undercooked. Check again in about five minutes.

Grain Pie

How such an ordinary sounding name hides such an extraordinarily good dessert! The "grain" in this pie refers to soft wheat kernels, and the pie is nothing more than a variation of the Ricotta Pie, above. But a word of warning: Buy grain that's distinctly labeled "soft" wheat. I've tried making this with hard wheat. Sorry, no amount of soaking or simmering will make those kernels palatable. If you use hard wheat, it will be inedible, your teeth will break, and a bad time will be had by all.

Grain Pie is Ricotta Pie with a sweetened crust, with orange blossom water for flavoring, and with the addition of the grain and some candied fruit as well.

A day before you make this pie, take two handfuls of the wheat kernels (about one-quarter cup, no more) and set them aside to soak in a bowl of warm water. Then, just before you start making the pastry dough, put the grain in a small pot, add two cups of water and a tablespoon of sugar and let the grains simmer slowly for about 20 or 30 minutes. They're ready when they are still springy to the tooth but no longer hard.

As with Ricotta Pie, we will need an 8 inch springform pan, or, if you'd prefer to leave it in the pan once it's done, a deep 9-inch pie pan.

Take one-and-a-half level cups of unsifted flour and add one-half teaspoon salt. Add one-half cup of sugar. Into this cut 10 tablespoons of cold butter. As always, this can be done with a pastry cutter or with a wide tined fork or, as we now do, in a food processor. When combined, the flour/butter/sugar mix should be grainy, not smooth.

To this add two beaten egg yolks and two to three tablespoons ice-cold water. Form this into a ball and set aside about a quarter of the total for the lattice top. Chill both pieces in the fridge for a half-hour.

Next, heavily flour a board or counter-top and a rolling pin. The dough will be very soft. Roll it out and line the interior of the springform pan or pie dish. Patch all holes. (A word of caution: Because this dough is almost a cookie dough more than a simple pie dough, it will try to pull apart and it will make holes. It's just that way; as holes appear, just patch them with a dab of more dough.)

For the filling, take about one-and-a-half pounds of ricotta cheese. Add to this the cooked and drained wheat grains, one-quarter cup flour, one-quarter teaspoon salt, the grated peel of one orange, one or two tablespoons orange blossom water, and one-half cup candied orange peel, lemon peel or citron — or any combination. (If the candied peel has been around for a while and is hard or sugary, soak it in warm water or some liquor for a while. None of this need be terribly exact.)

From here on in, the recipe is the same as for Ricotta Pie: beat four eggs until light and foamy and add one cup of sugar. Combine the sugar-egg mixture with the ricotta cheese-grain-candied fruit mixture and blend until smooth.

Pour the filling into the pastry-lined springform pan or deep pie dish. Roll out the saved pastry dough and, with a serrated-edge pastry cutter, cut the dough into inch wide, ten-inch-long strips. Crisscross the top of the pie with these strips to make a neat lattice.

Place the pie in a pre-heated, 350° oven and bake for 50–60 minutes. As with Ricotta Pie, the aim is to come out with a moist (not dry, not runny) cheesecake. After about 45 minutes test the center of the cake with a cake-tester or broom straw. If the tester comes out wet, the cake is still undercooked. Check it again in a few minutes.

Chestnuts

I've always thought of chestnuts as a minor pain in the neck – time consuming, difficult to shell, and often not terribly tasty. But when they are good, they're fine. We served them during the holidays with a big bowl of mixed nuts and seasonal fruits – including persimmons, one of this country's most underrated foods.

First, pick the chestnuts carefully. Look for shiny, large, unblemished nuts. If there's any hint of mold on any one, reject them all. Don't try to "find a few good ones." You'll fail utterly.

Now, on the round side of each nut cut an "X" with a sturdy sharp knife. A pocket-knife works fine, so long as it's sharp. Work with care, since one slip can cause a nasty slice in you instead of the chestnut.

Now, put the chestnuts in a bowl of water and let them soak for a few hours. Drain them and place them on a sheet of aluminum foil in a baking pan. (I suggest the aluminum foil since chestnuts, as they cook, tend to discolor whatever surface they rest on. This way, you just throw away the foil.) Roast them at 325–350° for 15 or 20 minutes. After this time, test one to see if they're done.

The problem with chestnuts is that they have not one shell, but two. The outer, hard shell is easy to remove, but the papery inner shell sometimes sticks to the nutmeat like it was epoxied. And sometimes it insinuates itself into the inside ridges of the nut. This wouldn't be so bad if it didn't taste so dreadful – like oak leaves. In fact, they're so full of tannin that that's exactly what they're like. The soaking we did before roasting was meant to help this peel away, but it doesn't always.

You can also let the nuts dry for a week or so before soaking and roasting. This seems to help with peeling, but it also gives the little buggers time to convert their sugars into starch, so they wind up tasting mealy and floury rather than sweet and, well, nutty. See why I have reservations about chestnuts?

Candied Orange Peel

If you'd like to make your own candied peel, one that actually tastes of orange, it's not that hard. (Time consuming, yes, but not hard.)

To make about two cups, peel three good-sized oranges and cut the peel into strips. This is the whole peel, white pith and all. (Perhaps easiest of all, cut cold oranges in half, juice them, drink the juice for your breakfast, and eat or discard the pulp remaining in the half shells.)

In a saucepan large enough to hold all the strips of peel, cover the peel with cold water, bring it to a boil, and simmer gently for five to ten minutes. Drain, rinse under cold water, and do this at least three times.

The aim is to leach out the bitter oil and soften the peel to prepare it to receive the sugar.

After the peel has been simmered, drained, and rinsed at least three times, set it aside. For every cup of cut peel you started with, bring one cup of sugar and a half cup of water to a boil in a saucepan. Once the sugar-water mixture has cleared and is about to come to a boil, add the peel and simmer it very gently until the inner peel begins to be translucent, about 30 minutes.

Once the peel has a slight clear sugar glaze to it, remove it from the syrup and drain it thoroughly on a rack. When cool, dust it with superfine sugar (sometimes called bar sugar), let the pieces dry individually and thoroughly, then put them aside in a container in the cupboard and use as needed.

A fine treat is to melt some chocolate to dip half of each peel in. These are nice sweets to put on your cookie tray when serving tea or coffee to guests. Or, better, to eat in the kitchen with your kids when they come home from school with a good report.

You can make your own bar sugar by putting a cupful of regular sugar in the blender and grinding it up for a few seconds.

(Late in life, I've learned how to "temper" chocolate. We never once dreamed of doing any such thing in the old neighborhood, but today the internet will tell anyone how to do it. If you master it, your dipped peels will have the sheen and snap of the finest Swiss chocolates.)

Ice

Lemon Ice

This stuff is so amazingly good that you wonder why we were ever allowed to have it. We never called it lemon ice; we just called it "Italian Ice." The man at the counter scraped it out of large containers, packed it into small accordion cups, and handed it over to us for a nickel. You squeezed the cup as it got to the bottom; it always made a mess, but it was worth it.

The same thing can easily be put together at home. You can give some to the kids after school or serve it in paper cups to guests standing around the deck after a barbecue, or you can even serve it up fancy, like a "French sorbet," after an elegant dinner. It's still just Italian Ice, and there's nothing better.

So, to begin. In a saucepan, combine two cups of sugar, the grated rind of one lemon and four cups of water. Bring the mixture to a boil and boil for five minutes, stirring so that all the sugar is fully dissolved. Remove the syrup from the heat and let it cool. Add three-quarters of a cup of freshly squeezed lemon juice. Pour this into a metal bowl and put it in the freezer. Every 20 minutes or so, whisk it to break up the ice crystals. In a few hours, depending on how cold your freezer is, you will have perfectly frozen lemon ice.

This will keep for a day or two in the freezer, but its grainy consistency suffers the longer it's held.

Orange Ice

This seems not to be as authentic as lemon ice, but it's every bit as good. In a saucepan combine two cups of sugar, the grated rind of two oranges, and four cups of water. Boil this for five minutes, stirring so that all the sugar is fully dissolved. After this syrup cools, add the juice of six oranges and the juice of one lemon. Continue as for lemon ice.

A non-traditional but most elegant way of serving this as a dessert is to pack the ice back into the orange shells you used for juice. Here's how: Instead of cutting the oranges in half for juicing, just cut off the top third. Now, carefully, without breaking the rind, juice each part of each orange. After juicing, while the ice is freezing, clean the pulp from the inside of the orange rinds. Chill these in the fridge until the ice is ready to serve and then fill and mound the larger part of each orange with the ice, laying the smaller piece a-swagger on top. Garnish with a mint sprig and serve right away. You may have to shave the bottom of each orange cup to help it sit steadily on the plate

Conclusion

Even though this book is a small snapshot of Italian-American city cooking during the better part of the 20th century, resist the temptation to look at it as merely a history text. It's a living tradition that, in its general elements, carries on through today. Sure, the empty lots where you might go to pick wild dandelion are probably gone from where you live. But that doesn't mean you can't buy dandelion greens these days at the fancy greengrocer in the upscale shopping mall. I know that few of you will saw through a piece of dried stockfish and soak it for a week or buy a hank of hog casings and make your own sausage. But some of you will, and that's good. Besides, once you eat homemade sausages, I do not believe you will ever again eat the chemically preserved, water-sodden, filler-laden, salty horror that passes for Italian sausages in your ordinary supermarket.

In that sense, this type of cookbook can be corrupting — it can bring you back to basics in a way that makes the jar of store-bought tomato sauce or the tube of pre-made polenta seem simply wrong.

But, yes, tastes change; and I have no doubt that some things in this book seem distinctly out of another culinary era. I rarely make pasta fazool or escarole soup anymore; our tastes change. Not only that, but we as a country have grown into increased food sophistication: There's so much more to choose from these days than tomatoes, olive oil, garlic, and basil. The cooking of just a few years ago has a way of seeming artless, simple, dated. But just as there are "back to basics" movements in everything from education to religion to child-rearing, so too in food does the circle tend to come 'round. When it comes around for you, then go back this book again.

But more: This book is not meant to be an end but a starting point. Move on from here to French and Asian cooking; move on from here to new and much fancier Italian dishes. Our forbearers may have been stuck, cooking and eating only what they knew. While they may have perfected what they knew, still all cuisines carry with them their own limitations – they are grounded in custom and habit and constrained by the familiar. But we, in today's America, are not so bound. We can, literally, have it all. In America, all peoples are here, all ingredients and foods are here, and all manner of cookbooks are here. Cave hominem unius libri, the priests taught us in high school – "Beware the man of one book." That advice goes in spades for cookbooks. When it comes to cooking and cookbooks, be omnivorous!

About the Author

Photo by Gerard Marandino

John Agresto still doesn't know what to do with his life. He's been a university professor of political science, history, and literature; he's been president or chancellor of three universities; he's been a fellow and scholar at various think-tanks; he spent time in Iraq and Kurdistan helping them to rebuild their system of higher education; he started an educational consulting company; he served in DC as the chairman of a federal agency; he was a county judge in New Mexico, where he still lives; and he is the author or editor of eight books ranging from works on education, politics, and law to cooking. Lately widowed, he was married for 55 years to his wife Cathy. Despite all that, he looks forward to his tombstone reading, simply, *"John Agresto — Gourmet, Raconteur, Bon Vivant, and Friend."*

www.ingramcontent.com/pod-product-compliance
Lightning Source LLC
Chambersburg PA
CBHW081442070526
44586CB00019B/2199